T0328608

Cambridge Elements ≡

Elements in Applied Linguistics
edited by
Li Wei
University College London
Zhu Hua
University College London

TRANS-STUDIES ON WRITING FOR ENGLISH AS AN ADDITIONAL LANGUAGE

Yachao Sun
Duke Kunshan University

Ge Lan
City University of Hong Kong

CAMBRIDGE
UNIVERSITY PRESS

Shaftesbury Road, Cambridge CB2 8EA, United Kingdom

One Liberty Plaza, 20th Floor, New York, NY 10006, USA

477 Williamstown Road, Port Melbourne, VIC 3207, Australia

314–321, 3rd Floor, Plot 3, Splendor Forum, Jasola District Centre,
New Delhi – 110025, India

103 Penang Road, #05–06/07, Visioncrest Commercial, Singapore 238467

Cambridge University Press is part of Cambridge University Press & Assessment,
a department of the University of Cambridge.

We share the University's mission to contribute to society through the pursuit of
education, learning and research at the highest international levels of excellence.

www.cambridge.org
Information on this title: www.cambridge.org/9781009532853

DOI: 10.1017/9781009336659

When citing this work, please include a reference to the DOI 10.1017/9781009336659

First published 2024

A catalogue record for this publication is available from the British Library.

ISBN 978-1-009-53285-3 Hardback
ISBN 978-1-009-33669-7 Paperback
ISSN 2633-5069 (online)
ISSN 2633-5050 (print)

Trans-studies on Writing for English as an Additional Language

Elements in Applied Linguistics

DOI: 10.1017/9781009336659
First published online: May 2024

Yachao Sun
Duke Kunshan University

Ge Lan
City University of Hong Kong

Author for correspondence: Yachao Sun, ys302@duke.edu

Abstract: This Element charts the historical development of trans-concepts in writing studies and scrutinizes the discussions surrounding translingual and second language (L2) writing. It further examines the emerging trends within trans-studies on writing and highlights the implications that trans-pedagogies hold for English as an Additional Language (EAL) writing. The Element consists of five key sections: (1) the evolution and enactment of various trans-concepts in writing studies; (2) the concerns and debates raised by L2 writing scholars in response to these trans-terms; (3) a response to these reservations through a bibliometric analysis of current research trends; (4) the potential variations in trans-practices across different contexts and genres; and (5) the role of trans-pedagogies in facilitating or potentially hindering the process of EAL writing teaching and learning. This Element serves as a resource for EAL writing educators by providing a comprehensive understanding of the potential benefits and challenges associated with trans-pedagogies.

Keywords: translanguaging, translingual practice, translingual approach, English as an additional language, writing

ISBNs: 9781009532853 (HB), 9781009336697 (PB), 9781009336659 (OC)
ISSNs: 2633-5069 (online), 2633-5050 (print)

Contents

1 Conceptualization of Trans-terms in Writing Studies

Over the last two decades, a novel perspective has emerged within the sphere of writing, specifically focused on trans-approaches. This includes concepts such as translanguaging (Creese & Blackledge, 2010; García, 2009; García & Li, 2014), translingual approach (Horner, Lu, et al., 2011; Lu & Horner, 2016), translingual practice (Canagarajah, 2013a; De Costa et al., 2017; Xie & Sun, 2023), translingual disposition (Lee & Jenks, 2016; Lu & Horner, 2013), and transmodality (Hawkins, 2018; Sun et al., 2021). These concepts have been discussed and enacted in different academic fields, including composition studies (Bou Ayash, 2016; Horner, Lu, et al., 2011), applied linguistics (Canagarajah, 2015; Li, 2018), TESOL (Flores & Aneja, 2017; Sun & Lan, 2021a), bilingual education (García & Li, 2014; García et al., 2017), and EAL/second language (L2) writing (Atkinson & Tardy, 2018; Gevers, 2018). Key principles underpinning these trans-approaches to writing, such as advocating for writer agency, viewing heterogeneity as the norm, and challenging monolingualism, have found widespread acceptance. These ideas have been put into practice across diverse contexts (such as English as a Second Language (ESL), English as a Foreign Language (EFL), and Foreign Language (FL) settings) and writer groups (e.g., ESL, Heritage Language, and FL learners) (Sun, 2022). The adoption of these principles serves diverse purposes, from understanding writing practices and improving pedagogy to facilitating teacher education (Sun & Lan, 2021a). These trans-terms respond to the rapid internationalization of writing education and enable a contextualization of writing practices based on rhetorical situations (such as context, audience, and purpose). These terms have their own conceptual roots and developmental trajectories, and three of them, that is, translanguaging, translingual approach, and translingual practice, are gaining increased attention within the field of writing studies (Sun & Lan, 2021b). Hence, to grasp a comprehensive understanding of trans-studies on writing, the following sections will individually introduce these three core trans-terms.

1.1 Translanguaging

The term *trawsieithu*, originally coined in Welsh by Cen Williams (1994), advocates for the simultaneous use of English and Welsh in classroom settings to maximize teaching and learning effectiveness. This term later underwent translation into English as "translanguaging" by Baker (2001), a term designed to encapsulate pedagogical practices involving diverse language resources. Translanguaging has been further developed into a practical and theoretical concept by Ofelia García, Li Wei, and their colleagues, who conceptualize it to understand the process of meaning-making with a variety of language and semiotic resources. Otheguy et al. (2015) propounded translanguaging as "the deployment of a speaker's full linguistic repertoire without regard for watchful adherence to the socially and politically defined boundaries of named (and usually national and state) languages." (p. 283). This definition challenges monolingualism and supports a decolonized perspective of language practices. Building upon these discussions, translanguaging has evolved into a process of knowledge construction that crosses named language boundaries, social and political constructs, and disciplinary conventions (García & Li, 2014; Li, 2018; Li & García, 2022). From a translanguaging viewpoint, an individual possesses an integrated linguistic repertoire rather than separate language systems and meshes various language resources in this repertoire to make meaning. The notion of viewing languages as static, discrete, and monolithic is problematic as it forms social and cognitive boundaries in the learning process by separating the target language from others. Therefore, multilingual students should be encouraged to use their entire linguistic repertoire creatively and critically for learning.

As a result of expansive discussions, translanguaging has been conceptualized and implemented in varied ways. Cenoz and Gorter (2017) differentiated translanguaging into pedagogical and spontaneous translanguaging. They argued that pedagogical translanguaging, initially employed in Welsh contexts, alludes to planned teaching practices that use diverse language resources and instructional strategies to cross language boundaries. On the other hand, spontaneous translanguaging is unplanned, fluid, and discursive, which typically occurs in natural contexts and can be strategically harnessed for pedagogical goals. These translanguaging practices, both inside and outside the classroom, help create a translanguaging space "by bringing together different dimensions of their personal history, experience, and environment; their attitudes, beliefs, and ideology; and their cognitive and physical capacity into one coordinated and meaningful performance, transforming language learning and language use into a lived experience." (Li & Ho, 2018, p. 38). In other words, this translanguaging space is created by the spontaneous assembly of individual, social, and ecological resources in situ. From a pedagogical standpoint, this translanguaging space encompasses teachers' translanguaging stance (language ideologies and teaching beliefs for instructional practices), translanguaging design (planned teaching practices based on students' language repertoires), and translanguaging shifts (the strategic response to students' language practices during instruction) (García et al., 2017). As a common feature of multilinguals' language practices, translanguaging has been increasingly used within and beyond language classrooms to activate students' full linguistic repertoire for learning.

The growing interest in translanguaging, both theoretically and practically, has spurred scholars to link it with critical pedagogy. Poza (2017) reviewed translanguaging research and contended that "[w]e should expect that translanguaging would be positioned as a tool, both for improving educational outcomes, and for asserting and creating identities, as well as for questioning and subverting hegemonic linguistic norms." (p. 117). Thus, he recommended, "connect[ing] translanguaging to an educational and social justice agenda of critical pedagogy that challenges contemporary linguistic norms and the ideologies of race, state, and/or colonial subjectivity in which these norms are grounded." (p. 118). This critical approach to translanguaging or critical translanguaging has been further elaborated to challenge hegemonic norms and raise awareness of language hierarchies and power dynamics in sociolinguistic spaces (Hamman, 2018). Turner and Lin (2020) argued that "the naming of languages needs to be incorporated into translanguaging theory in a way that acknowledges the social construct or 'named languages' as integral to the expansion of one's repertoire as a whole." (p. 423). Hence, named languages are vital for critical translanguaging to recognize linguistic hierarchies and destigmatize minority/indigenous languages. However, named languages should be viewed as fluid, hybrid, and negotiated entities rather than as fixed, discrete, and monolithic ones. Recent reviews of translanguaging research (Cinaglia & De Costa, 2022; Sah & Kubota, 2022) echo these discussions and underscore the importance of adopting translanguaging critically to resist nationalist and neoliberal ideologies that perceive language learners from a deficit perspective and safeguard historically marginalized languages, cultures, and identities by incorporating named languages into translanguaging theory and practice.

The recent decolonial agenda of translanguaging research (García et al., 2021) has followed this critical approach to translanguaging to champion social, cultural, political, and linguistic justice. Li and García (2022) stated that translanguaging is "intended as a decolonizing project, that is, a way to undo the process through which the knowledge base and linguistic/cultural practices of colonized people was obliterated. In so doing, translanguaging opens spaces for social and cognitive justice in the education of these students." (p. 2). In this respect, translanguaging contests colonial/dominant norms and promotes justice by viewing all languages and cultures as assets rather than obstacles to learning. This decolonial perspective has been advanced by discussing translanguaging assessment (Lee, 2016; Steele et al., 2022) for linguistic social justice, which "confront[s] the inequitable discursive economies that afford disproportionate amounts of social capital to certain language practices over others." (Lee, 2016, p. 176). Translanguaging assessment questions language "standards" and calls for increasing teachers' and students' awareness of linguistic inequality in education. Canagarajah (2022), based on his personal translanguaging practice experiences, discussed the meanings and challenges of decolonizing linguistics and argued that meanings should be negotiated based on rhetorical situations rather than fixed by language ideologies, grammatical structures, and "native speaker" communities. These studies challenge norms constructed from and through colonization and advocate for decolonizing language and education by understanding and practicing them based on dynamic and complex contexts.

As the term translanguaging continues to undergo theorization and implementation, it has garnered increasing attention in various academic fields, such as bilingual education, sociolinguistics, applied linguistics, and TESOL. Meanwhile, it has been employed in empirical writing studies as a theoretical or pedagogical framework to investigate the impact of different language and semiotic resources on the writing process. However, translanguaging is seldom conceptualized in these studies as a term to corroborate or refine the understanding of writing (Sun & Lan, 2021b). One primary reason is that translanguaging does not signify an endpoint or end product, although it can embody the evolving process leading to outcomes such as translations or written pieces (Baynham & Lee, 2019; Domke, 2023; Sato & García, 2023). Another reason is that translanguaging (indicated by its suffix -ing) emphasizes on-the-spot interactions between speakers or speakers and nonhuman tools (such as digital translators and dictionaries); therefore, it is considered the overarching communicative skill of multilinguals (Canagarajah, 2011a). This is in contrast to writing, which often caters to an asynchronous audience rather than an immediate one. Consequently, writing scholars have gravitated toward the terms "translingual approach" and "translingual practice" to advocate for a more inclusive view of writing that challenges monolingual norms and biased perceptions.

1.2 Translingual Approach

The concept of a translingual approach emerged in the field of writing studies, most notably through the influential work of Horner, Lu, Royster, and Trimbur, whose seminal paper "Language Difference in Writing: Toward a Translingual Approach" was published in 2011 in *College English*. Three key principles underpin this approach, namely empowering all writers, especially those who are minoritized, marginalized, or labeled, acknowledging linguistic heterogeneity as the norm rather than the exception, and challenging monolingualism that regards languages as static, discrete, and monolithic linguistic entities. These guiding tenets arose from a comprehensive investigation into language and language difference (Horner, Lu, et al., 2011; Horner & Tetreault, 2017).

A translingual approach builds upon the work that has argued for the validation of nondominant English varieties, such as African American Vernacular English (AAVE), in academic writing. This advocacy can be traced back to the 1974 Conference on College Composition and Communication statement, *Students' Right to Their Own Language* (SRTOL), in which writing scholars argued for students' rights to employ their unique English varieties/dialects for academic purposes and resisted a deficit-oriented perspective of minoritized English varieties. The principle of viewing prestigious English dialects critically in academic contexts, such as Edited American English (EAE) and Standard Written English (SWE), has been widely accepted, as demonstrated in various classrooms. For instance, Young's (2004) concept of codemeshing challenged the compartmentalization of English varieties based on context, such as using EAE/SWE in school settings and AAVE at home. Arguing that this bifurcation does not reflect the language use realities of multidialectal/multilingual writers, he called for the legitimization of AAVE in academic writing. This line of inquiry informs the development of a translingual approach to writing.

Apart from English variety studies, a translingual approach also draws from research on language difference. While SRTOL addressed the right of students to use their English varieties, it gave less attention to other languages in academic writing. Horner (2001) argued that multilingual writers' existing language and cultural knowledge should also be seen as resources rather than hindrances in academic settings. Therefore, language difference studies in TESOL and L2 writing (e.g., Matsuda, 1999; Silva, 1997) provide important implications for developing a translingual approach to writing. Silva (1997), for instance, proposed an ethical approach to ESL writers to resist a deficit approach to ESL writing and writers. He elaborated on ethics as "a system or code of conduct" (p. 359) and contended that ESL writers should be treated from four aspects, that is, "they need to be (a) understood, (b) placed in suitable learning contexts, (c) provided with appropriate instruction, and (d) evaluated fairly." (p. 359). Twenty years later, Tardy and Whittig (2017) extended these principles to English as an additional language (EAL) writers and added a fifth aspect to advocate for writer agency. Other studies in L2 writing (e.g., Matsuda, 1999; Silva, Leki, and Carson, 1997) contested monolingual, monocultural, and ethnocentric approaches to advocate for more inclusive writing environments. These studies challenge English monolingualism in writing studies, advocate for an open and inclusive attitude toward unconventional language use in academic writing, underscore writer agency in shaping language with multilingual writers' own language and cultural resources, regard difference as a resource rather than a deficit, and consider heterogeneity as the norm. These perspectives are critical to conceptualizing a translingual approach to writing (see Horner & Tetreault, 2017).

The increasing attention to language and language difference and the rapid development of globalization in writing studies have motivated scholars to reconsider how languages and language varieties function in the writing process from translingual perspectives. The concept of contact zones, "social spaces where cultures meet, clash, and grapple with each other, often in contexts of highly asymmetrical relations of power, such as colonialism, slavery, or their aftermaths as they are lived out in many parts of the world today" (Pratt, 1991, p. 34), has been broadly referenced to construe how power relations between language resources affect meaning negotiation and construction. This concept challenges monolingualism and views heterogeneity as the norm of communication in communities and societies. Grounded on this concept, Lu (1994) proposed a multicultural approach to writing to illustrate and exemplify how language resources are synergistic for meaning-making. The phrase, "can able to," used by a Malaysian Chinese student in her classroom, showcased the agentive use of language resources (Chinese and English) in contact zones. This phrase reflects three conflicting meanings of "can" and "able to" generated from the positions of an "English native speaker," a dictionary, and an ESL student writer. The "English native speakers" in her classroom viewed this structure as an error based on those students' language knowledge; the random house dictionary showed that "can" had one more meaning than "to be able to," that is, "have permission to"; and the ESL student considered this structure a rhetorical expression for negotiating and constructing meaning in a specific context through text. In Lu's (1994) words, this structure connotes "ability from the perspective of external circumstances" (p. 452) and manifests writer agency in shaping their own language. These studies challenge a monolingual approach to language difference and advocate for a dynamic, synergistic, and negotiated orientation to language, language difference, and language use, which foregrounds a translingual approach to writing.

Understanding language resources as synergistic rather than separate for meaning-making has enlightened scholars to question the English-only policy in writing education. The English-only policy has long dominated writing studies (Horner, 2001). Horner (2001) argued that the English-only policy deriving from cognitive and structural approaches to writing education fails to "understand language as material social practice" (p. 742), i.e., language is contingent on purpose, audience, and context rather than fixed linguistic structures, in that cognitive approaches regard language learners as deficient language users and linguistic structural approaches render unconventional language structures as errors. To challenge the English-only legislation in writing studies, Horner and Trimbur (2002) reviewed the English-only debates in US writing studies and criticized English monolingualism, territorialization, and reification of languages. They stated that English-only or English monolingualism fails to respond to the internationalization of writing studies and the dynamics of globalization. Horner, Lu, and Matsuda (2010) took a step further toward the challenge of monolingualism in writing studies. They contended that the English-only policy permeated US society and higher education undervalues language and cultural resources that multilingual and multicultural students bring to the classroom and underestimates the complexity and variability of students' language use. In addition, the English-only policy, according to them, undermines indigenous languages and cultures by viewing language learners as deficient language users; therefore, they call for resistance to English-only legislation and an open and inclusive attitude toward language diversity in society in general and in higher education in particular. The challenge to English monolingualism in writing studies has become one of the central tenets of a translingual approach to writing, which helps develop a critical agenda for translingual research on writing.

In line with these discussions, Horner, Lu, et al. (2011) proposed a translingual approach to writing with three main principles, that is,

> (1) honoring the power of all language users to shape language to specific ends; (2) recognizing the linguistic heterogeneity of all users of language both within the United States and globally; and (3) directly confronting English monolingualist expectations by researching and teaching how writers can work with and against, not simply within, those expectations. (p. 305)

These translingual principles have been widely accepted and enacted in writing classrooms worldwide. To understand a translingual approach comprehensively, Horner, NeCamp, and Donahue (2011) discussed and distinguished a monolingual, a traditional multilingual, and a translingual approach. They argued that monolingual and traditional multilingual approaches rooted in a monolingual approach are problematic in that they view language as static, discrete, and monolithic and consider a multilingual as multiple monolinguals in one. Instead, a translingual approach regards language as fluid, synergistic, and negotiated and sees a multilingual as a unique person with multiple language resources for meaning-making. Therefore, they called for implementing a translingual approach in writing studies by motivating teacher-scholars to learn additional languages, encouraging individuals, institutions, journals, and conferences to have a more inclusive, open attitude toward language difference, and urging writing scholars and practitioners to view heterogeneity as the norm of language use. A translingual approach to writing has been further conceptualized (Lu & Horner, 2013; 2016) based on the aforementioned discussions. In short, a translingual approach to writing that integrates the ideas from the studies of language/language difference, contact zones, and English-only debates views writing as performative, synergistic, emergent, contingent, ideological, and contextual.

1.3 Translingual Practice

Another pivotal term that has made its mark in writing studies is translingual practice, which was proposed by Liu (1995) to delve into the literature, national culture, and translated modernity in China between 1900 and 1937. Subsequently, the term was further developed and refined within writing studies as a means to highlight the fluidity, hybridity, and negotiability of various semiotic resources, such as languages, colors, images, and symbols, used for meaning-making. Suresh Canagarajah, through his substantial contributions (2013a; 2015; 2018), has been instrumental in further shaping and refining the concept of translingual practice within writing studies. Hence, this section primarily focuses on the evolution of this term as delineated in Canagarajah's body of work. However, it is crucial to acknowledge that other scholars such as De Costa et al. (2017), Jain (2014), and Lee and Jenks (2016) have also made contributions to the understanding of translingual practice by conducting empirical research in diverse contexts to study this phenomenon in action.

Translingual practice, as a language use phenomenon, has been a societal mainstay for a long time and has garnered increased attention over the past two decades. As a concept, translingual practice has been primarily developed from a critical perspective to illustrate the relationship between multilingual writers and the academic community. Canagarajah (2002) elucidated this relationship by exploring different approaches to EAL education, such as English for Academic Purposes (EAP), Contrastive Rhetoric (CR), Social Process (SP), Transculturation Model (TM), and Contact Zones. These approaches serve to delineate how multilingual writers navigate the divide between their vernacular and academic communities. Canagarajah critiqued the EAP approach, which perceived the academic community as a homogenous entity with distinctive discourse characteristics, for reinforcing the boundaries between multilingual writers' vernacular and academic communities. The EAP approach's rigidity, as he claimed, left little room for unconventional language use and restricted resource utilization from outside the academic community. Similarly, while the CR approach respected the boundaries between vernacular and academic communities, it treated culture as static and homogeneous, which limited the potential for crossing community boundaries despite its apparent respect for difference. The SP approach, on the other hand, promoted traversing across community boundaries for meaning-making. However, it viewed the discourses of communities as discrete, thereby underestimating the complexity of multi-lingual writers and their communities. The TM approach offered flexibility in blurring boundaries and allowing multilingual writers to employ their vernacular resources in academic settings. However, it failed to account for the power dynamics at play in academic practices, such as the strict gatekeeping policy in scholarly publications. With these limitations in mind, Canagarajah (2002) advocated for a contact zones approach to raise awareness of the power relations between communities and encourage multilingual writers to creatively and critically shuttle between communities. This approach promotes the utilization of multilinguals' own language, social, cultural, and ideological resources in academic contexts. These ideas contribute to the foundational understanding of translingual practice and serve as the bedrock for its conceptualization.

Expanding on the critical view of the community, a negotiation model has been applied to understand language use in writing. The traditional monolingual approach to writing has been critiqued for its inherent limitations, as Canagarajah (2006b) articulated that it "conceive[s] literacy as a unidirectional acquisition of competence, preventing us from fully understanding the resources multilinguals bring to their texts" (p. 589). This critique suggests that a monolingual approach fails to capture the full spectrum of abilities and resources that multilingual writers can offer. To address this, Canagarajah (2006b) proposed a negotiation model based on an analysis of a Sri Lankan senior professor's academic writing in different languages, Tamil and English in that case, for different purposes such as local and international publication. The negotiation model centers on the study of multilingual writers' movement between languages, their process of writing in diverse languages, the resources they derive from their own languages and cultures, the adaptation of these resources to contextual changes, and their agency in navigating between discourses to achieve their communicative goals. He contended that the most important factor in these texts was not language or culture but the rhetorical situation. Therefore, he advocated for multilingual writers to be allowed to use multiple, not just dominant, language and cultural resources to meet their communicative objectives in varying rhetorical situations. Canagarajah (2007) further evolved this negotiation model into a practice-based model aimed at redefining language acquisition. This redefinition was constructed based on discussions about dichotomies prevalent in second language acquisition (SLA) studies, such as grammar versus pragmatics, determinism versus agency, individual versus community, purity versus hybridity, fixity versus fluidity, cognition versus context, and monolingual versus multilingual acquisition. He posited that "[l]anguage acquisition is based on performance strategies, purposive uses of the language, and interpersonal negotiations in fluid communicative contexts."

(p. 936), thus framing language as performative, emergent, and contingent. These studies challenge conventional constructs of form, cognition, and language acquisition in both writing and SLA studies and emphasize the importance of negotiation between languages and language users when creating meaning in ever-changing social and ecological contexts.

The conceptualization of translingual practice has been informed by research on codemeshing. This term, initially coined by Young (2004), advocates for the inclusion and mixing of diverse dialects and registers in academic writing. Young's argument is centered around "allowing black students to mix a black English style with an academic register . . . This technique not only links literacy to black culture, it meshes them together in a way that's more in line with how people actually speak and write." in that "true linguistic and identity integration would mean allowing students to . . . combine dialects, styles, and registers." (p. 713). Therefore, codemeshing challenges conventional, rigid writing approaches and promotes the process of interweaving various codes. Canagarajah (2006a) expanded on Young's concept of codemeshing in his discussion of the role of World Englishes (WE) in writing studies, thereby challenging monolingualism and advocating for a pluralization of academic writing. He put forth that the hybrid use of WE and SWE should be considered a legitimate expression of the individual voice in academic writing. To illustrate this point, he explored the textual and pedagogical potential of integrating AAVE and SWE for academic purposes. To further elaborate on the concept of codemeshing in the context of multilingual writing, Canagarajah (2009) provided an analysis of strategies multilingual individuals used to negotiate differences and discussed the applicability of conversational strategies to written discourse. He explored tactics such as the co-construction of intersubjective norms (norms collaboratively established by multilingual speakers during conversation), the use of hybrid codes for communication (including languages and language varieties), fostering a consensus-oriented and supportive interaction among multilingual speakers, and integrating various semiotic resources (such as language, environment, social context, and gestures) for meaning-making. He then further examined these strategies in the context of a literacy narrative by one of his students, Buthainah. In the analysis, he demonstrated how the strategic use of Arabic, English, and emoticons in Buthainah's writing underscored the importance of considering languages beyond the dominant one as valuable resources rather than obstacles. He further encouraged students to leverage all available resources for academic purposes. Canagarajah (2009) posited that codemeshing is not just multilingual but also multimodal— employing visual, aural, and tactile modalities. He advocated for the appreciation of multilingual strategies, empowerment of multilingual individuals to shape their own language use, openness toward and inclusion of language differences, and a critical approach to handling errors in academic writing.

Drawing upon translanguaging research (refer to 1.1 of this section), code-meshing is regarded as "the realization of translanguaging in texts," while translanguaging itself is seen as "the general communicative competence of multilinguals" (Canagarajah, 2011a, p. 403). Canagarajah (2011b) encapsulated the primary assumptions of translanguaging as follows: (1) languages are integrated rather than separate in one's repertoire; (2) languages constitute merely one aspect of one's repertoire; (3) multilingual competence arises from the interplay and negotiation of multiple languages; (4) competence does not consist of isolated competences for different languages but a unified multicompetence that encompasses all languages in one's repertoire; and (5) multilingual proficiency is the capacity to adapt the use of different languages to various rhetorical situations rather than mastering each language in its entirety. He asserted that, despite its primary focus on conversation, translanguaging holds the potential for understanding language use in the writing process. He instantiated it by analyzing Buthainah's hybrid use of languages such as English, Arabic, and French and visual symbols such as motifs (͡ ☺ ̮ ☺ ̮ ☺ ̮͡)), emoticons (☺), and elongations (doon't) in her text. Through this lens, translanguaging provides a more encompassing comprehension of the multilingual writing process by viewing all codes or semiotic resources as part of a cohesive system for expressing one's voice. Guided by this perspective, Canagarajah (2011a) outlined pedagogical strategies for integrating translanguaging in the writing process, including recontextualization, voice, interactional, and textualization strategies. According to him, recontextualization strategies equip multilingual writers to negotiate difference by considering audience, genre, and purpose. Voice strategies empower them to decide on the manner and extent of codemeshing based on their individual interests and identities. Interactional strategies facilitate the co-construction of meanings with their readers, while textualization strategies motivate multilingual writers to utilize various resources for different purposes across diverse contexts. These studies show that research on codemeshing and translanguaging in writing predominantly focuses on the visible integration of different language and other semiotic resources in the writing process or within the text.

Grounded on the aforementioned discussions, the concept of translingual practice has been proposed. Canagarajah (2013a) theorized translingual practice by exploring and comparing various emerging theoretical orientations, such as integrationist linguistics, the school of language ideology, the contact zones perspective, communities of practice, dynamic systems theory, and the sociocognitive perspective. He maintained that translingual practice underscores the hybridity, fluidity, and negotiability of diverse semiotic resources engaged in the process of meaning-making. Canagarajah (2015) further articulated that translingual practice "perceives a synergy between languages which generates new grammar and meanings . . . transcends individual languages, and goes beyond language itself to include diverse modalities and semiotic systems . . . reminds us that language and meaning are always in a process of becoming, not located in static grammatical structures" (p. 419).

Essentially, translingual practice is a dynamic, emergent, adaptive behavior that allows individuals to align with the perpetually evolving social and ecological world. Building upon this understanding, Canagarajah (2018) illustrated translingual practice as spatial repertoires. This idea modifies Pennycook and Otsuji's (2015) concept of spatial repertoires, which "link[s] the repertoires formed through individual life trajectories to the particular places in which these linguistic resources are deployed" (p. 83). Canagarajah's modification extends "beyond the methodological individualism, human agency, and verbal resources the definition favors. Spatial repertoires may not be brought already to the activity by the individual but assembled *in situ*, and in collaboration with others, in the manner of distributed practice" (p. 37, emphasis in original). This expanded understanding of spatial repertoires implies that repertoires are not just what individuals bring to specific places in response to corresponding activities; rather, they are collaboratively, contingently, and emergently constructed through the synthesis of individual life trajectories, associated others, and temporal–spatial elements such as time, space, surrounding environments, and physical materials. Consequently, Canagarajah (2022; 2023) characterizes translingual practice as a diverse, resistant, and creative communicative practice that works toward decolonizing linguistics and politics. Within this context, language carries its own norms, which are sedimented over time, but these norms are not fixed as language constantly co-constructs meaning alongside other resources in varying times and spaces. These perspectives underscore that the contemporary notion of translingual practice emphasizes the importance of spatial materials, diminishes or decentralizes the roles of language and human agency in meaning-making, and views writing as a process of assembling spatial repertoires.

1.4 Summary

This section traces the evolution of three main concepts within trans-studies on writing, specifically translanguaging, translingual approach, and translingual practice. Each possesses its own theoretical origins and historical trajectories, yet they converge on several core principles. Horner (2018) delineated six key commonalities among these concepts as they diverge from monolingual ideologies:

> First, they signal the presence of more than one language as the norm of communicative situations. Second, they signal the fluidity of the defining identities and relations among these languages. Third, they position language use as entailing the mixing and changing of different languages, and, fourth, and relatedly, they grant agency to language users to do so, rather than seeing such mixing and changing as evidence of linguistic failure, incompetence, or threat. Fifth, they posit the identities of not only individual languages but also individual language users as fluid. Finally, they locate language not outside material social history but in material social practices as the always emerging outcome of language practices rather than the universals against which language practices are to be measured. (Horner, 2018, pp. 78–79)

Essentially, these concepts have emerged as responses to the rapid evolution of globalization within language and writing studies. They highlight heterogeneity, emphasize the contingent and emergent nature of language, promote a more inclusive attitude toward language difference, challenge the monolingual paradigm in language teaching and research, and treat additional languages as resources, not obstacles, in teaching, learning, and using a target language. The prefix 'trans-' used in this element embodies these shared principles.

Despite their substantial overlaps, translanguaging, translingual practice, and translingual approach each exhibits distinct nuances. Translanguaging, primarily emerging from the field of bilingual education, is marked by its focus on simultaneous interactions among language users or between these users and tools such as digital translators. This concept does not indicate any end products, such as translations or written texts. Instead, it represents an evolving, dynamic process, potentially leading to such end products, thereby highlighting the fluid and continuous nature of language interaction and learning. In contrast, translingual practice, which synthesizes perspectives from sociolinguistics, literacy, and writing studies, underscores the synergy of linguistic and semiotic resources in both the writing process and the written products (such as codemeshing). Slightly different from the practical orientations of translanguaging and translingual practice, translingual approach, with its roots in composition studies, places more emphasis on language ideology. It delves into the perceptions and values associated with language and language use and focuses more on the reflective exploration of language ideologies. In the subsequent section, we will delve deeper into how the trans-terms have been met with concerns from L2 writing scholars.

2 Concerns about Trans-approaches to Writing

Trans-approaches have begun to permeate a multitude of writing-related research domains, including basic writing (Horner, 2011), genre approach to writing (Bawarshi, 2016), writing assessment (Dryer, 2016; Lee, 2016), reading and writing (Trimbur, 2016), language ideology and policies in writing (Kilfoil, 2015), writing and transfer (Leonard & Nowacek, 2016), writing teacher education (Canagarajah, 2016; Flores & Aneja, 2017), Writing across the Curriculum (WAC)/Writing in the Disciplines (WIC) (Horner, 2018), and L2 writing (Atkinson & Tardy, 2018; Sun & Lan, 2021b; 2023; Sun et al., 2023). Grounded in postmodern, poststructural, and postcolonial theories, trans-studies have critically examined traditional perceptions of language, language difference, language use, language user, and context to advocate for blurring the strict boundaries, which reflects on trans-practices' synergistic, emergent, and contingent characteristics inherent in meaning-making. Such explorations have offered valuable insights to writing researchers and practitioners by urging a reevaluation of writing norms and the interplay between dominant languages and other languages in the landscape of writing research and education. For instance, conventional norms are revealed to be not rigidly presupposed but rather social constructs open to change. Writing researchers and educators are encouraged to embrace a broader acceptance of students' unconventional language use in academic writing. Furthermore, languages other than the target one are not seen as hindrances but are recognized as valuable resources for writing. These fundamental principles of trans-approaches to writing have garnered broad acceptance. However, they are not without their critics and have generated some concerns. This section seeks to summarize some of these key concerns, including the overemphasis on language performance, the flattening of language differences, and the downplaying of language norms and writing conventions. By doing so, it provides a balanced overview of the ongoing debates in this rapidly evolving research area.

2.1 Overemphasizing Language Performance

One of the concerns raised about trans-approaches to writing pertains to an overemphasis on language performance. Trans-approaches tend to focus on the performative aspect of language, paying attention primarily to the audible and visible aspects of the writing process and the final text. Matsuda (2014) critiqued it by arguing that the emphasis on visibility neglects the potential subtleties of negotiation, where the writer may opt for an apparently dominant choice. He stressed that, in translingual writing practices, the negotiation process itself, often invisible, is as crucial as the visible product. Therefore, a narrow view focused on the end result may overlook less obvious negotiation manifestations or situations where writers choose not to deviate from dominant practices (pp. 480–481). This sentiment was echoed by Cook (2022), who remarked that translanguaging should not only be about what can be seen or heard and critiqued the implicit assumption in translanguaging that "if a language cannot be seen or heard, it is not there." (p. 56). He described it as only the visible tip of the iceberg and asserted that languages, even when not immediately perceptible, cannot be "turned off" in our minds; their availability can only be moderated. These discussions underscore a significant issue: the tendency of trans-approaches to writing to overlook the invisible aspects of language use. Examples of these invisible aspects include the historical development of a language, language users' emotions, motivations, and identities, as well as the differences in language competence among individuals. Kramsch (2018) highlighted a similar point, noting that the term "temporal" in trans-theories tends to overlook the historical aspect and the passage of time, instead favoring visibility – a "space of appearance" (p. 110–111). She contended that this visual bias could risk excluding those elements that lie beyond the reach of the visual frame, such as language competence that reflects the mental ability to use, shuttle, or orchestrate language resources. Further, Gilyard (2016) disputed the view of languages as mere abstractions and emphasized that people do possess language competencies that enable language performances, even though these competencies are challenging to study as they reside in the brain's regions (p. 287). He argued that an overemphasis on performance, coupled with an underestimation of individual competence in trans-studies on writing, could impede critical discussions on the similarities and differences among languages, language users, and contexts.

To elaborate on the performative nature of language and language use, competence has been reconceptualized in trans-studies on writing. Pratt et al. (2008) introduced the notions of translingual and transcultural competence as a means to re-envision the roles of college and university foreign language departments. They delineated translingual and transcultural competence as "the multilingual ability to *operate between languages*" (p. 289, emphasis in original) to stress the importance of embedding language studies within cultural, historical, geographic, and cross-cultural contexts. By doing so, students are encouraged to grasp the disparities in interpretations, mindsets, and worldviews across different languages. Pratt and colleagues asserted that including transcultural subject matter and fostering translingual reflections in foreign language instruction would heighten students' skills in transitioning between languages and cultures. The form of competence they discussed emphasizes "the powers of the intellect and the imagination, the ability to reflect on one's place in the world with depth and complexity, and understanding of the degree to which culture and society are created in language" (p. 288). This implies the mental capabilities of multilinguals to operate between languages and cultures, which aids in expanding their perspectives and fostering a critical comprehension of the world. Subsequent trans-studies on writing have advanced these concepts further. For instance, Horner, Lu, et al. (2011) posited that competence should encompass more than mastering language forms or conventions; instead, it should involve the modifications and innovations that multilingual individuals bring to language use. As such, they defined competence as the capacity to both command and amend language conventions to suit intricate contexts. Additionally, Canagarajah (2013a) drew on the concept of alignment from Atkinson et al. (2007) and Atkinson (2011) to lend a trans-perspective to the understanding of competence. Defined as "the complex means by which human beings effect coordinated interaction, and maintain that interaction in dynamically adaptive ways" (Atkinson et al., 2007, p. 169), alignment provided a fresh outlook on competence. Canagarajah (2013a) maintained that the "meaning-making potential of language and human competence emerges through processes of alignment and adaptation and does not reside in the system of language or cognition" (p. 32). From these trans-perspectives, it is clear that language is not just a linguistic competence fixed within the stable grammatical systems of human brains but a performative act rooted in fluid and complex sociocultural contexts. These conceptions of competence in trans-studies on writing further emphasize the performative aspect of language and highlight the risk of neglecting the historical evolution of language and its users.

The performative approach to understanding language and language difference highlights the in situ assembly of spatial repertoires. However, this perspective often neglects the historical aspect of writing development, a critical dimension that reflects the individual and sociocultural differences between languages and their usage. It is this historical component that provides essential context to writing phenomena. Kramsch (2018) argued that

> language is not only a social semiotic that brings humans and other inhabitants of the planet together but a historical institution that we have constructed precisely to deal with the ethical, legal, and political aspects of our life together. As an institution language ensures continuity, mutual intelligibility, and understanding, but it also preserves our uniquely human capacity to embrace both the thrills of space and the vulnerabilities of time. (p. 114)

From this perspective, language possesses both performative and historical features that illuminate the inception, development, transformation, and even disappearance of diverse writing styles, strategies, and pedagogies. Such illumination can strengthen our understanding of the field of writing and propel it forward in a more informed manner. Therefore, scholars have advocated incorporating the historical development of language into trans-studies on writing. Gevers (2018), for instance, examined the pedagogical and ideological constraints of trans-approaches to writing and argued that those invested in trans-pedagogies, including writing instructors and teacher-scholars, need to acknowledge the distinct developmental characteristics of spoken and written forms. This recognition would better enable students to employ language use based on genre, purpose, and context. Similarly, Atkinson and Tardy (2018) elucidated the relationships between L2 writing, trans-studies on writing, and written corrective feedback (WCF) and underscored the importance of considering multilingual students' language development in writing education. Echoing these insights, Arnold (2020) warned that reliance on visible language differences or performative language in trans-pedagogies might inadvertently fortify monolingual viewpoints and misguide writing teachers and students. These studies not only encourage more attention to the historical development of language and its differences over an excessive focus on language performance but also prompt caution against deficient approaches to language and language difference that are derived from historical biases and prejudices in trans-studies on writing.

The overemphasis on language performance within trans-studies on writing has elicited a growing concern about ignoring power relations and social inequality. Both Flores (2013) and Kubota (2016) raised critiques about the trans-turn in TESOL and applied linguistics, noting that this turn runs parallel with the rise of neoliberalism. Flores (2013) argued that the trans-turn serves political and economic agendas, thus erasing the language history of nation-states and subaltern societies. He championed the need to pay greater attention to power dynamics and social inequalities within TESOL at both the institutional and individual levels. Kubota (2016) expressed similar sentiments and stated that the trans-turn promotes plurality, hybridity, and fluidity but simultaneously ignores marginality, inequality, and linguistic imperialism. She referred to this turn as the celebration of "neoliberal multiculturalism," which valorizes "individualism, difference-blindness, and elitist cosmopolitanism rather than critical acknowledgement of power" (p. 487). Consequently, she warned that "[c]oncepts such as hybridity and cosmopolitanism can undermine the positive effects of rootedness to form local solidarity among minoritized groups, and instead promote neoliberal capitalism" (pp. 482–483). She also called for an increased focus on power relations and social inequality within applied linguistics. These perspectives are supported by recent reviews such as those by Cinaglia and De Costa (2022) and Sah and Kubota (2022), which underline the importance of a critical approach to trans-studies on writing. Such an approach can help resist nationalist and neoliberal ideologies while empowering historically marginalized languages and language users in academic contexts. These discussions suggest that while research on language performance is crucial to challenging structural and monolingual ideologies, an overemphasis on performance could lead to neglecting invisible aspects, such as language competence and historical development. These hidden factors are essential for understanding the power dynamics between languages and their users. While competence – intrinsically tied to history – may not fully explain performance, it can shed light on why individuals perform differently in the same space and at the same time. Still, there remains a debate on how competence interacts with multiple languages. Various theories exist, such as whether languages exist within a single mind and community (Cook, 2016; 2022), within a unified repertoire (García & Li, 2014; Li, 2018; Li & Zhu, 2013; Otheguy et al., 2015), within an integrated multilingual system (MacSwan, 2017; 2022), or within an evolving repertoire, where the overlap between first and second languages increases as proficiency grows (Rinnert & Kobayashi, 2016). Therefore, the overemphasis on language performance remains a central concern that necessitates further exploration and discussion within the domain of trans-studies on writing.

2.2 Flattening Language Differences

Another critique of trans-approaches to writing pertains to the flattening of language differences, which implies a homogenization of language uses as equally different in every temporal-spatial context. Scholars such as Lu and Horner (2013) have argued for a temporal-spatial frame to treat elements such as language, users, practices, conventions, and contexts not as separate, pre-existing, stable entities but as perpetually emergent and mutually constitutive (p. 587). Similarly, Canagarajah (2018) advocated for the transcendence of boundaries (such as language, social, cultural, geographical, and disciplinary) and the transgression of powers (e.g., linguistic, political, and human) to understand the process of meaning-making from a poststructural perspective. He emphasized that every communicative act is an assemblage of spatial repertoires, i.e., a synergy of semiotic resources, artifacts, and environmental affordances. They all work together in a specific time and space for a particular purpose. In this frame, languages and humans are simply parts of this assemblage. From a temporal-spatial standpoint, all writing can be deemed translingual, and all writers can be considered translingual writers since writing as a performance for negotiating and constructing meaning is always rooted in temporal-spatial locations. However, this perspective can inadvertently result in the flattening of language differences. Gilyard (2016), grounded in his experiences in language teaching and usage, critically examined the primary principles of trans-approaches to writing. He argued that treating language as an abstraction could lead to the flattening of language differences, thereby undermining critical and informed discussions about language similarities and differences. He defined this flattening of language differences as emphasizing the assemblage of spatial repertoires while neglecting individual, historical, sociocultural, and political differences pertinent to language and its users. Similar concerns were also evident in Milson-Whyte's (2013) analysis of the work of Jamaican multilingual students in US classrooms. She raised three issues regarding trans-practices in multilingual contexts: i.e., "problems regarding valorizing, yet not legitimizing, minoritized languages; problems arising from language users' inability to code-switch effectively; and the potential for ignoring sameness and difference while attempting to address difference in language use" (p. 115). The ignoring of language similarities and differences – or what Gilyard (2016) also refers to as the "sameness of difference" (p. 286) – results in the flattening of language differences in trans-studies on writing.

The flattening of language differences, instead of facilitating the crossing of disciplinary boundaries, might intensify disciplinary divisions. Language differences, encompassing linguistic, social, cultural, and individual aspects, have been extensively explored and debated. Many ideas that underpin trans-approaches to writing, such as challenging monolingualism, asserting writer agency, and acknowledging heterogeneity as the norm, are not new to writing studies (Matsuda, 2013, 2014; Severino, 2017). A consequence of flattening language differences is that it potentially obscures the understanding of an issue from relevant disciplinary perspectives, which could not only hinder the bridging of divides but also exacerbate disciplinary divisions, such as those between composition studies and SLA (Tardy, 2017). Matsuda (2014) associated the flattening of language differences with the overuse of trans-terms and warned that "[i]nflating a term and concept has serious consequences —the term can lose its descriptive and explanatory power, leading to the trivialization and eventual dismissal of the concept. Overextending a term makes it vulnerable to co-option by contrary ideological positions" (p. 478). Consequently, flattening language differences could result in misunderstandings concerning the relationship between writing terms, such as "translingual writing" and L2 writing. Matsuda (2014) noted that the concept of translingual writing was not always fully understood, and some researchers used it "not for its intellectual value but for its valorized status." (p. 479). Moreover, he stated that trans-ideas, which have been extensively discussed in fields such as descriptive linguistics, historical linguistics, and sociolinguistics, are often loosely connected and "not fully or accurately represented in the discussion of translingual writing" (p. 479). Severino (2017) similarly argued that translingual writing, which borrows ideas from SLA and L2 writing, often conflates the two concepts. For instance, Tannenbaum (2014) defined translingual writing as "writing in a language different from one's mother tongue" (p. 99), a definition typical of L2 writing. Drawing from her learning experiences of writing in Spanish (advanced level) and Chinese (beginning level), Severino (2017) emphasized the importance of acknowledging varying degrees of language differences and individual proficiency levels, which are often overlooked in trans-studies on writing. These discussions suggest that the flattening of language differences might do more harm than good, potentially exacerbating rather than mitigating disciplinary divisions.

The flattening of language differences has raised concerns about the unitary perspective on writing embraced by trans-approaches. In order to highlight the emergent, contingent, and negotiable nature of language in the process of meaning-making, trans-scholars, such as Canagarajah (2015) and Horner, NeCamp, and Donahue (2011), distinguished trans-approaches from both monolingual and traditional multilingual approaches (see Section 1). Trans-approaches, they proposed, perceive languages as intertwined within a unified repertoire rather than separate entities within distinct cognitive systems and regard language competence as holistic across all languages rather than discrete competencies for individual languages. In this sense, language use is seen as an assemblage of all available language resources, language acquisition is conceptualized as multidirectional rather than linear, and language users are understood as unique individuals who construct meanings with language resources in an agentive, creative, and critical manner. Thus, in contrast to monolingual and traditional multilingual approaches, trans-approaches understand writing as performative, emergent, contingent, ideological, and contextual (Horner & Tetreault, 2017; Lu & Horner, 2016). This integrated perspective on language and language use has been labeled as a "unitary model of multilingualism" (MacSwan, 2017; 2022), which is contentious. MacSwan (2022) critiqued that "[r]egardless of how we approach an explanation of the patterns, the analysis will inevitably incorporate categories expressing linguistic discreteness. These empirical observations are sufficient to refute ... [the] claim that bilingual grammar is unitary, disaggregated and internally undifferentiated" (p. 95). This unitary perspective, which considers all language users as identical translinguals and all forms of writing as indistinguishable translingual writing, causes the flattening of language differences. MacSwan (2017; 2022), instead, advocated for a multilingual viewpoint on trans-approaches and asserted that languages and grammatical resources are both shared and discrete. He contended that "[w]e are not all individually *monolingual*, but rather *multilingual*, with rich internal diversity; as with any person in any community, the richness of the linguistic diversity of multilingual students should be viewed as a critically important resource for promoting their educational success" (MacSwan, 2022, p. 108, emphasis in original). Therefore, language differences, whether they are linguistic, individual, sociocultural, or historical, should not be flattened but valued; nonetheless, these differences should not be perceived as static and deficient.

The flattening of language differences has been met with critiques by various scholars in the field of writing, as aforementioned. These critiques address a variety of concerns, including the historical aspects of language within nation-states and subaltern societies (Flores, 2013), the issues of marginality, inequality, and language imperialism (Kubota, 2016), the complexity of language sameness and difference (Gilyard, 2016; Matsuda, 2013; Milson-Whyte, 2013), a neologism for existing ideas (Tardy, 2017), term inflation and linguistic tourism (Matsuda, 2014), ignoring of language learning experiences (Severino, 2017), missing discussion of language development (Atkinson & Tardy, 2018), and a lack of discussion of language proficiency (Matsuda, 2014; Severino, 2017). To address these critiques, trans-scholars have introduced concepts such as translation (Horner, 2017; Horner & Tetreault, 2016), postcolonial ideology (Canagarajah, 2017; Cushman, 2016), and spatial repertoires (Canagarajah, 2018) to underscore that trans-approaches do not dismiss the existed boundaries and powers of named languages, but rather they emphasize the transcendence of those boundaries and transgression of those powers in writing. However, these responses often overlook the individual differences in the cognitive transformation of sociocultural heritage and the sociohistorical differences between named languages. Ignoring these differences could discourage discussions about similarities and differences between languages and language users. Terms reflecting sociohistorical differences among writers and writing, such as L1, L2, ESL, EFL, EAL, and Generation 1.5, may be viewed as problematic when interpreted as implying cognitive deficits or any forms of deficiency. However, these terms can also facilitate understanding of the similarities and differences between named languages and their users concerning their historical, social, cultural, ideological, and educational backgrounds. Therefore, language differences need to be reconsidered in trans-studies on writing. This reconsideration should not only challenge monolingualism, advocate for writer agency, and aim to decolonize language education but also value these differences for a more comprehensive understanding of writing phenomena.

2.3 Downplaying Language Norms and Writing Conventions

The impact of overemphasizing language performance and flattening language differences within trans-approaches, particularly for students still accommodating language norms and writing conventions, is increasingly being scrutinized in writing education. Ferris (2014) conducted a review of three influential books: *Cross-Language Relations in Composition* (Horner, Lu, & Matsuda, 2010), *Shaping Language Policy in the U.S.* (Wible, 2013), and *Writing in the Devil's Tongue* (You, 2010). While acknowledging that these texts shared a philosophical stance challenging monolingualism's problems, she argued that they did not sufficiently address practical pedagogical implications for teachers in the classroom. In a related discussion, Atkinson et al. (2015) elaborated on the relationship between L2 writing and translingual writing in an open letter to writing studies editors and organization leaders by articulating their overlapping areas and distinct facets. They also expressed concerns about the adequacy of translingual writing in preparing students for success in their academic lives. Echoing these pedagogical worries, Matsuda (2014) cautioned against the potential for "linguistic tourism" in trans-approaches to writing pedagogies. He defined linguistic tourism as an intellectual curiosity-driven fascination with the unfamiliar, which results in the selection of attractive but unrepresentative linguistic features in teaching and learning an additional language. While some trans-studies on writing (Canagarajah, 2015; Horner, 2018) have attempted to address these concerns by illustrating how trans-approaches could enhance and refine writing pedagogies, their primary emphasis is on advocating for writer agency through resistance to rather than accommodation of dominant language norms and writing conventions. This emphasis on resistance tends to downplay language norms and writing conventions that are crucial for student writers' academic success. Research (e.g., Arnold, 2016, 2020; Bou Ayash, 2016; Kato & Kumagai, 2022; Kuteeva, 2020) has revealed students' concerns about the practicality of nonconventional language practices in high-stakes writing scenarios, such as exams and job or graduate school applications. There are also concerns about the negative implications of deviating from language norms and writing conventions on their language proficiency, competence, and identity, and about the potential marginalization of students who do not possess the same local languages. These studies highlight the importance of incorporating language norms and writing conventions in a manner that expands multilingual students' linguistic repertoires. This incorporation can allow students to use these resources more critically and agentively to challenge deficit approaches to EAL writing and writers and have a more nuanced understanding of their trans-practices.

In trans-studies on writing, it is essential to engage thoughtfully with established language norms and conventions, even as their boundaries are critically examined. Trans-approaches are distinguished for their emphasis on blurring, softening, or even transcending the set boundaries between named languages (e.g., English and Spanish), language varieties (e.g., SWE and AAVE), and language contexts (e.g., ESL and EFL). Despite this boundary-challenging focus, linguistic categorizations remain indispensable for analyzing language performance and competence during the writing process and in the written product. Therefore, scholars such as MacSwan (2017, 2022) prefer a multilingual lens on trans-concepts to value language boundaries while also pushing against them. Illustrating this concept, Canagarajah's (2013b) examination of a student's usage of four sets of trans-strategies – envoicing, recontextualization, interaction, and entextualization – showcases how these methods can simultaneously accommodate and challenge linguistic boundaries. He illustrated envoicing strategies as allowing writers to employ various semiotic resources to convey their identities and voices, especially in linguistically diverse contexts. Recontextualization strategies, he argued, refer to producing a text to fit genre and communication requirements. These strategies help writers adapt their messages according to audience expectations, especially when shared values are not assumed. Interaction strategies emphasize the collaborative effort in meaning-making, which is essential when shared language backgrounds are absent. Entextualization strategies are about how text creation, from drafts to revisions, can assist and guide reader's interpretations. Together, these strategies offer a comprehensive way for writers to clarify, negotiate, and construct meanings based on different rhetorical situations.

Canagarajah (2013b) asserted that these strategies helped students to "find the right balance between authorial intentions and community expectations, writers' voices and readers' uptake, writerly designs and audience collaboration" (p. 64). In other words, it is critical to navigate language norms and writing conventions with agency and critical thought based on specific rhetorical situations. The long-standing tradition of challenging linguistic boundaries has deeply informed writing research and education. A plethora of research, including studies on L2 writing, composition, and applied linguistics (Silva & Leki, 2004), L2 writing and basic writing (Matsuda, 2003), L2 writing and SLA (Manchón, 2016; Manchón & Williams, 2016; Ortega, 2012), L2 writing and reading (Carson & Leki, 1993; Hirvela & Belcher, 2016), and L2 writing and composition studies (Horner, Lu, & Matsuda, 2010; Horner & Tetreault, 2017; Matsuda, 1999), substantiates that language norms and conventions should not be downplayed in that they serve as bridges that allow multilinguals to cross rather than ignore a diverse range of boundaries.

Diminishing the importance of language norms and writing conventions may lead writing instructors and students to conflate the concept of trans-approaches to writing with codemeshing (see Section 1.3). Canagarajah (2013b) explained codemeshing as "a form of writing in which multilinguals merge their diverse language resources with the dominant genre conventions to construct hybrid texts for voice" (p. 40). While trans-studies on writing often leverage the concept of codemeshing to challenge established language norms and conventions, the overreliance on it has raised questions about its utility in writing education (Gevers, 2018). This conflation has also led some researchers and practitioners to mistake codemeshing for trans-practices (Schreiber & Watson, 2018). Clarifying the distinction between codemeshing and trans-concepts, Canagarajah (2013a) posited, "while codemeshing often characterizes the end product of many multilinguals, translingual practice can lead to products approximating SWE also" (p. 188). Guerra (2016) further underscored this distinction by posing a rhetorical question: "when we as teachers take a translingual approach to difference, are we expecting students to produce a particular kind of writing that mimics what we call code-meshing, or do we want students to develop a rhetorical sensibility that reflects a critical awareness of language as a contingent and emergent, rather than a standardized and static, practice?" (p. 228). This rhetorical question stresses the value of fostering students' rhetorical sensibility over codemeshing when interpreting language and language differences through a trans-perspective lens.

Lu and Horner (2016) and Horner and Tetreault (2017) advocated a shift in focus within trans-approaches to writing by contending that the critical point is not the quantity of languages interwoven within a text but the manner and motivation behind how writers both adapt to and challenge language norms and writing conventions. Similarly, Leonard and Nowacek (2016) elucidated the relationship between transfer and trans-concepts and argued that trans-approaches are not only pertinent to writing skills but also bound up with rhetorical strategies that are used to make those writing skills visible and valuable. Gilyard (2016) supported this position and stated, "I would not expect students to mimic any specific strategy, so-called code-meshing or not, and that rhetorical astuteness is always the aim relative to emergent *and* standardized language, standardizing also being a process of emergence" (p. 286, emphasis in original). This statement underscores a movement within trans-studies on writing from a product-oriented focus to an emphasis on rhetorical awareness. Thus, the shifting focus from codemeshing to rhetorical sensibility represents a significant evolution within trans-approaches to writing, which signifies that trans-practices should not be viewed as a specific writing form (such as code-meshing) but rather understood as a rhetorical instrument to illuminate the negotiability, permeability, and fluidity of boundaries existing among languages, language users, and contexts.

2.4 Summary

The progressive understanding of language and language difference as fluid and hybrid has given rise to certain apprehensions regarding trans-approaches to writing. Critics express concerns about an overemphasis on language performance, the flattening of language differences, and the downplaying of language norms and writing conventions. Thus, the utility of trans-pedagogies in writing education, particularly for language learners, has been called into question (Atkinson et al., 2015; Atkinson & Tardy, 2018; Ferris, 2014; Gevers, 2018; Gilyard, 2016; Matsuda, 2014; Milson-Whyte, 2013). In this section, we have summarized some of these specific issues surrounding trans-approaches to writing. As mentioned earlier in this section, to address these concerns, concepts such as translation (Beiler & Dewilde, 2020; Horner & Tetreault, 2016), decolonial (Canagarajah, 2022; García et al., 2021), and critical (Cinaglia & De Costa, 2022; Sah & Kubota, 2022) have been adopted to highlight that trans-approaches to writing do not dismiss the existence of named languages and their inherent linguistic, sociocultural, and historical differences. Instead, they emphasize the negotiability and permeability of these differences. Based on these discussions surrounding trans-concepts, we adopt the term 'trans-' to describe the individual deployment of a variety of language resources for meaning-making and knowledge construction, akin to the concept of "idiolect" as described by Otheguy et al. (2015). Conversely, we employ 'multilingual' to refer to the external categorization of languages, which includes the social, cultural, political, historical, and educational frameworks that define named languages. Trans-approaches to writing continue to be developed and refined, with criticisms and concerns serving as guiding influences. These ongoing adjustments aim at implementing trans-pedagogies in the writing classroom in a more critical manner. This iterative process ensures the development of trans-approaches to be increasingly reflective and responsive to these critiques.

3 A Bibliometric Analysis of Trans-studies on Writing

This section introduces a bibliometric analysis of studies on trans-approaches to writing. In light of the extensive conceptual debates surrounding trans-concepts and related concerns, as outlined in previous sections, it becomes important to delve into inductive and data-driven analyses. The bibliometric analysis serves as an effective approach to survey the landscape of this research area and provide tangible insights that might respond to these concerns. This section will begin with a general introduction to bibliometric analysis and its relevance. This will be followed by an exploration of important bibliometric analyses in the field of applied linguistics to offer a context within which trans-approaches to writing are situated. We then shift our focus specifically to recent bibliometric studies concerning the trans-approaches to analyze the current state of research in this area and to highlight the research methods used in our bibliometric analysis. The subsequent presentation and discussion of our bibliometric results will address the concerns previously mentioned to contribute empirical perspectives to the debates in trans-studies on writing. Lastly, the section will conclude with a consideration of the implications of these findings for future trans-studies on writing.

3.1 Bibliometric Analysis and Applied Linguistics

Bibliometrics, initially proposed by Pritchard (1969), is a research approach that applies statistical methods to evaluate scientific publications. Sometimes used interchangeably with scientometrics in library science, bibliometrics originally focused on the analysis of research productivity –measured by, for example, the number of publications from institutions – and research impact, gauged by the number of times a publication has been cited (Lei & Liu, 2019a). The bibliometric practice has resulted in a collection of citation indices in library science, including but not limited to the Book Citation Index (BCI), Conference Proceedings Citation Index (CPCI), Science Citation Index (SCI), Social Science Citation Index (SSCI), and Arts and Humanities Citation Index (AHCI). From these indices, the Impact Factor (IF) has been developed as a measure of the average frequency with which articles from specific journals are cited within a particular year. For instance, in 2022, the *Applied Linguistics* journal had an impact factor of 4.155, which implies an annual average of 4.155 citations per article published in that year. It is generally perceived that journals with higher impact factors exert a greater influence within their respective fields. Recognizing the utility of bibliometrics, its application has expanded from its original scope in library science to various other fields, including applied linguistics. Particularly in the last two decades, including the 2010s and 2020s, applied linguists have increasingly acknowledged the benefits of this approach. As a result, there has been an increase in bibliometric studies aimed at analyzing knowledge development, research trends, and research productivity of scholars across different areas within applied linguistics (Sun & Lan, 2021b). The utilization of this approach in trans-studies on writing offers a promising avenue for capturing comprehensive insights into the evolving research landscape of this area.

The application of bibliometric studies in applied linguistics has been a relatively recent trend, primarily conducted after 2015. The work of Lei and Liu (2019a) probed into research trends in applied linguistics based on publications from 2005 to 2016. Their comprehensive delineation of the bibliometric methods adopted in their study provided a path for other researchers to replicate such analyses. Subsequently, this research approach has been utilized to delve into an array of research areas within applied linguistics. As Sun and Lan (2021b) enumerated, these areas include but are not limited to applied linguistics in general (Lei & Liu, 2019a), research articles within a specific journal such as *System* (Lei & Liu, 2019b), and various subfields within applied linguistics such as EAP (Hyland & Jiang, 2021), multilingualism (Lin & Lei 2020), Chinese as a second language (Gong et al. 2018), L2 writing (Sun & Lan, 2023), translanguaging and translingualism (Sun & Lan, 2021b; Sun, Wang & Qin, 2024), and computational linguistics (Liao & Lei, 2017). In terms of their objectives, these bibliometric studies reveal the research productivity of individual scholars, the research impact of institutions and journals, and prevailing research trends within applied linguistics. The value of bibliometrics, as demonstrated by these studies, lies in its ability to quantify research productivity, impact, and trends. Such studies have the potential to supplement or corroborate research syntheses to have a comprehensive view of a given research area. Hence, it becomes evident that bibliometrics should be given greater consideration within the realm of applied linguistics due to its comprehensive analytical capabilities. It is this belief that inspired us to undertake the current bibliometric analysis of trans-studies on writing to have a big picture of this research area and identify research trends to respond to the aforementioned debates.

3.2 Bibliometric Analysis and Trans-studies

The trans-concepts in this Element represent a focused area of study within applied linguistics and rhetorical and composition studies, encompassing translanguaging, translingual approach, and translingual practice (see Section 1). This research area has received increasing scholarly attention since the early 2010s. Horner, Lu, Royster, and Trimbur's (2011) opinion piece is viewed as a foundational work in trans-studies on writing. As a consequence of this contribution, trans-research on writing has witnessed rapid development in the past decade. This research area is a nascent yet rapidly expanding area of academic interest. Given its fast growth, a bibliometric analysis of the trans-studies on writing is necessary to provide fundamental bibliometric data, such as annual publication counts, for insights into the evolving research trends within trans-scholarship.

To our knowledge, only two bibliometric studies that focus on the trans-scholarship were published, each with distinct research focuses. The first study by

Sun, Wang, and Qin (2024) employed a bibliometric analysis to offer a comprehensive illustration of the evolution of translanguaging over the past two decades. Utilizing bibliometric data from the Web of Science, the study encompassed various analytical dimensions, such as the yearly count of scientific documents, the citation count of the documents, the sources and origins (affiliations and countries) of the documents, as well as prevalent keywords and research trends. The findings from Sun et al.'s (2021) study revealed that translanguaging scholarship had experienced rapid growth over the past twenty years, as reflected by the increasing annual document count up until 2021. Five leading contributing nations to the research on translanguaging were identified – namely, the United Kingdom, the United States, South Africa, Spain, and China. In addition, their findings also showed that the subject of translanguaging had been extensively explored within applied linguistics and second or foreign language education, as indicated by high-frequency keywords such as bilingual education, multilingual literacy, and multi-modality. The second study, conducted by Sun and Lan (2021b), is a bibliometric analysis highlighting trans-studies on writing between 2011 and 2020. Drawing from a corpus of 165 peer-reviewed journal articles, the study investigated three main aspects regarding the development of this research area, that is, highly cited authors, highly cited articles, and evolving research trends, as suggested by term usage. Influential researchers within this area included, among others, Suresh Canagarajah, Bruce Horner, Ofelia García, Paul Kei Matsuda, and Wei Li. High-impact publications included Canagarajah (2013a), Horner, Lu, Royster, and Trimbur (2011), and García and Li (2014). When it came to research trends, specific terms (e.g., translingual practice, translanguaging space, spatial repertoire) had seen an increase in usage, while others (e.g., codemeshing, monolingualism, code-switching) had witnessed a significant drop over the decade. These findings provide insight into the trajectory of trans-studies on writing from 2011 to 2020.

Sun, Wang, and Qin (2024) and Sun and Lan (2021b), both echoed a need for additional bibliometric exploration of trans-scholarship to corroborate the findings of their respective studies. We aim to respond to this call by undertaking an analysis of the extant body of work, specifically focusing on journal articles pertaining to trans-studies on writing. To supplement previous bibliometric studies, we decided to utilize a distinct dataset – the Scopus bibliometric dataset, which differs from those used by Sun et al. (2021) and Sun and Lan (2021b). In particular, our research addresses the following three questions:

1. What is the number of trans-studies on writing published each year?
2. What are the highly cited publications in trans-studies on writing?
3. What is the co-occurrence of keywords in trans-studies on writing?

3.3 Methods

We collected our bibliometric data from the Scopus database following three steps. In step one, we used the document search function to scan for specific keywords within the titles, abstracts, or listed keywords of the articles. Our search keywords fell into two categories, that is, various forms of the trans-terms (e.g., "translingual," "translingualism," and "translanguaging") and diverse variations of writing (e.g., "writing," "writings"). For step two, we refined our search parameters to only include the English language, final productions, and journal articles. With our keyword search, we located 238 documents, which we then downloaded as a CSV file. Step three involved a manual screening process. Given the relatively small volume of texts, we were able to individually scrutinize the abstract of each document in order to ensure that the articles specifically focused on trans-studies on writing as opposed to trans-research more generally. Through this process, we narrowed the dataset down to a representative collection of 190 journal articles.

For the data analysis process, we employed some semi-automated techniques due to the manageable corpus size of 190 journal articles. We used the "Sort & Filter" function in CSV to address research questions 1 and 2. To achieve this, we organized the bibliometric data first by publication year, which allowed us to count the number of annual publications, and then by citation numbers. This enabled us to identify and prioritize highly cited journal articles. To answer research Question 3, we utilized VOSviewer, a publicly accessible tool for bibliometrics. The bibliometric data, that is, the CSV file, was loaded into this tool. We then selected "co-occurrence" for the analysis type and "Author keywords" for the data to be analyzed. While we had the option to analyze different types of keywords (e.g., indexed keywords), we thought that author-identified keywords would provide a more accurate reflection of article content. VOSviewer permits the setting of a threshold, which is the minimum occurrence number for a keyword to be considered. We opted for the default threshold of "5" as the minimum number of keyword occurrences. Following the tool's guidelines, we generated the keyword analysis within VOSviewer (Waltman, Van Eck, & Noyons, 2010). By adhering to this systematic process, we were able to effectively answer all the research questions.

3.4 Results and Discussions

3.4.1 RQ-1: What Is the Number of Trans-studies on Writing Published Each Year?

Figure 1 (The number of published journal articles each year) offers a chronological view of the number of journal articles published annually from 2006 to the present day. The data from Scopus suggests a general upward trend in the publication volume of trans-studies on writing over this period,

PUBLICATION NO.

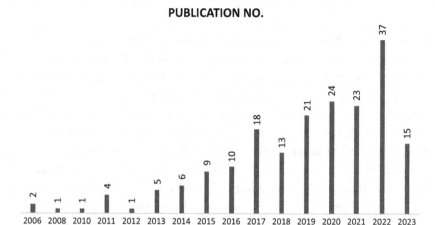

Figure 1 The number of published journal articles each year

Note. The bibliometric analysis was conducted in May 2023.

although the exact number of publications may exhibit minor fluctuations year on year. This increasing pattern of trans-publication can be broadly classified into four distinct stages. First, from 2006 to 2010, the volume of published journal articles was relatively scant. For instance, there were only two articles published in 2006 and a single article in 2008. During this stage, there were some years with no trans-studies on writing published at all, notably in 2007 and 2009. The second phase, spanning 2011 to 2015, shows an uptick in the number of published journal articles compared to the prior period, with, for example, six articles in 2014 and nine in 2015. The increased interest in trans-studies on writing during this phase could be led by two influential works: Horner, Lu, Royster, and Trimbur's (2011) "Language Difference in Writing: Toward a Translingual Approach," and Canagarajah's (2011a) "Codemeshing in Academic Writing: Identifying Teachable Strategies of Translanguaging." These publications are considered seminal works that significantly drew scholarly attention toward the trans-concepts within writing studies.

The third phase, extending from 2016 to 2018, shows a further surge in the volume of published journal articles, with numbers ranging between ten and twenty during these three years. Specifically, we observed ten articles in 2016, eighteen articles in 2017, and thirteen articles in 2018. This suggests that trans-studies on writing began attracting even more research interest during this period. Lastly, the phase from 2019 to 2022 witnessed publication numbers fluctuating between twenty and forty per year, with the peak reached in 2022 at thirty-seven publications. Of note is the year 2023, for which data until May already shows fifteen articles. With this promising start, we anticipate the total count by year-end to exceed thirty-seven. In sum, our analysis of the annual publication volumes aligns with Sun and Lan's (2021b) provisional three-stage overview of trans-studies on writing, namely the initiation stage (2011–2014), the development stage (2015–2017), and the extension stage (2018 to present). Our data further reveal an earlier phase (2006–2010), which can be designated as the "pre-initiation stage" of trans-studies on writing.

3.4.2 RQ-2: What Are the Highly Cited Publications in Trans-studies on Writing?

Utilizing data from Scopus, we focused our bibliometric analysis exclusively on published journal articles, excluding other types of publications such as books, book chapters, and conference proceedings. This analysis led us to identify the top ten most frequently cited articles pertaining to the topic of trans-studies on writing, which are listed in Table 1 (highly cited publications) alongside their respective authors, years of publication, and total citation counts. At the top of the citation is Canagarajah's (2011a) article, "Codemeshing in academic writing: Identifying teachable strategies of translanguaging," which has amassed a noteworthy 655 citations over the past 12 years from 2011 to 2023. Close to it, with 315 citations during the same time frame, is the 2011 collaborative piece by Horner, Lu, Royster, and Trimbur, entitled "Language difference in writing: Toward a translingual approach." We were not surprised by the prevalence of these two works in the citation counts relating to trans-studies on writing for two primary reasons. Firstly, these seminal publications have shaped the discourse in the trans-scholarship on writing, thereby earning their status as landmark studies. Secondly, our findings corroborate those of Sun and Lan's (2021b) study, which similarly identified these two articles as the most frequently cited during the 2010s in the realm of trans-studies on writing.

Further inspection of Table 1 reveals Velasco and García's (2014) piece, "Translanguaging and the Writing of Bilingual Learners," as the third most cited journal article with 214 citations since its publication. The table also lists other widely cited works, such as those by Canagarajah (2013b), Lu and Horner (2013), and Smith, Pacheco, and Almeida (2017). These results are echoed by Sun and Lan's (2021) study, which likewise recognized Canagarajah (2013b), Lu and Horner (2013), and Horner, NeCamp, and Donahue (2011) among the top-cited articles of the 2010s. Another article warranting particular attention is "Translanguaging and Literacies" by García and Kleifgen, published in 2020. Despite its relatively recent publication, it has already garnered 98 citations, placing it as the sixth most frequently cited article in our dataset. Remarkably, it is the only article published in the 2020s that has made it into the list of highly

Applied Linguistics

Table 1 Highly cited publications

Author	Article Titles	Year	Citation
Canagarajah S.	Codemeshing in academic writing: Identifying teachable strategies of translanguaging	2011	655
Horner B., Lu M.-Z., Royster J. J., Trimbur J.	Language difference in writing: Toward a translingual approach	2011	315
Velasco P., García O.	Translanguaging and the Writing of Bilingual Learners	2014	214
Canagarajah S.	Negotiating translingual literacy: An enactment	2013	156
Lu M.-Z., Horner B.	Translingual literacy, language difference, and matters of Agency	2013	102
García O., Kleifgen J.A.	Translanguaging and Literacies	2020	98
Horner B., NeCamp S., Donahue C.	Toward a multilingual composition scholarship: From English only to a translingual norm	2011	93
Smith B.E., Pacheco M.B., de Almeida C.R.	Multimodal codemeshing: Bilingual adolescents' processes composing across modes and languages	2017	73
Schreiber B.R.	"I am what i am": Multilingual identity and digital translanguaging	2015	72
De Los Ríos C.V., Seltzer K.	Translanguaging, coloniality, and English classrooms: An exploration of two bicoastal urban classrooms	2017	70

Note. Please see the APA citations of the journal articles in the reference list

cited articles, achieving this in less than three years. As such, it is reasonable to anticipate that García and Kleifgen's (2020) publication will continue to amass citations, potentially becoming one of the foremost highly cited articles in trans-studies on writing in the future.

Despite our identification of Smith, Pacheco, and Almeida (2017), Schreiber (2015), and De Los Ríos and Seltzer (2017) among the top ten most highly cited journal articles through our bibliometric analysis using Scopus data, these articles were not listed as such in Sun and Lan's (2021b) study. This discrepancy could be attributable to three primary factors. First, unlike our analysis which solely focused on journal articles, Sun and Lan's study encompassed a wider range of publication types, including books and book chapters, which may have altered the citation rankings. Second, Sun and Lan's analysis was restricted to the 2010s, while the three articles in question were published in 2015 and 2017. The relatively shorter span (3–5 years) leading up to 2020 might not have provided sufficient time for these publications to accrue a high number of citations. Finally, the methods of the two analyses differ fundamentally. While we employed Scopus data to track citation counts, Sun and Lan (2021b) analyzed the works referenced within the publications themselves. This difference in methodology should also be taken into account when comparing the two studies. These three factors contribute to the disparities observed between our bibliometric analysis and Sun and Lan's (2021b) findings.

3.4.3 RQ-3. What Is the Co-occurrence of Keywords in Trans-studies on Writing?

A keyword analysis is a crucial aspect of bibliometric research, which serves as a reservoir of the primary information embedded within research publications. As indicated by Guo et al. (2016), this type of analysis can offer insights into the prevailing research trends and dominant topics within a given field. Using VOSviewer for this task, we analyzed co-occurrences of keywords within trans-studies on writing, as gleaned from our Scopus data. Out of the 703 identified keywords, 21 met the minimum occurrence threshold of "5" and were therefore included in the visualization of the co-occurrence network in VOSviewer (refer to Figure 2 (Co-occurrence of keywords)). This visualization reveals five distinct, color-coded clusters within the trans-studies on writing, each signifying a significant correlation among the keywords contained therein (Shi, Miao & Si, 2019). These clusters, in turn, represent specific research topics within trans-studies on writing. The clusters comprise the following keywords:

- Cluster 1: translanguaging, translingualism, multimodality, literacy, L2 writing, identity, and English
- Cluster 2: writing, multilingualism, English language learner, language learner, and English learner, home language
- Cluster 3: translingual, translingual writing, translation
- Cluster 4: translingual practice, academic writing
- Cluster 5: bilingual, bilingualism, biliteracy

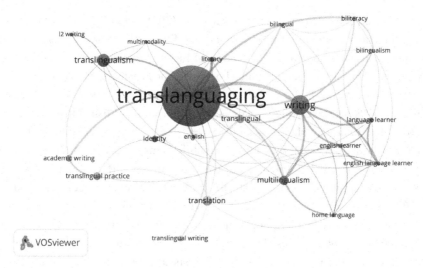

Figure 2 Co-occurrence of keywords

Further insights can be gleaned by examining the co-occurrence network of keywords. Beyond the five color-coded clusters, it is important to note the variation in node sizes. Each node's size signifies the frequency of the associated keyword's occurrence within our Scopus data. For instance, the largest node within the visualization corresponds to the keyword "translanguaging," which is the most frequently used keyword across all the data, with a total occurrence count of eighty-four. Other noticeably large nodes in the figure also highlight significant keywords within the trans-studies on writing. These keywords include, but are not limited to, the following:

- "Writing": the total occurrence = 27
- "Translingualism": the total occurrence = 18
- "Multilingualism": the total occurrence = 14
- "Translation": the total occurrence = 13
- "Translingual" and "translingual practice": the total occurrence = 12
- "Translingual writing": the total occurrence = 10
- "Academic writing": the total occurrence = 9

In addition to nodes, the co-occurrence network of keywords also features links connecting these nodes, each of which represents a keyword. These links symbolize the relationships between the keywords, with the size of each link denoting the strength of its corresponding relationship. A prime example is the robust connection between "translanguaging" and "writing," represented by the link with the greatest strength, quantified as "8." Other links between nodes within the figure, representing significant relationships among keywords, include but are not limited to the following:

- "Translanguaging" and "literacy": the link strength = 6
- "Multilingualism" and "writing": the link strength = 6
- "Translanguaging" and "academic writing": the link strength = 5
- "Translanguaging" and "biliteracy": the link strength = 5
- "Writing" and "language learner": the link strength = 5
- "Translanguaging" and "translingualism": the link strength = 4
- "Translanguaging" and "bilingualism": the link strength = 4
- "Translanguaging" and "multilingualism": the link strength = 4

The co-occurrence network of keywords provides valuable insights into the research trends in trans-studies on writing. It enables us to observe the key themes, topics, and relationships that underpin the current state and future direction of this research area. Regarding the noticeable themes and topics, the most frequently occurring keywords, such as "translanguaging," "writing," and "translingualism," indicate the primary foci in trans-studies on writing. The frequent co-occurrence of these terms suggests a vibrant research landscape revolving around the examination of language fluidity, language meshing, and how these trans-practices are applied within writing contexts. These dominant themes indicate an ongoing academic interest in the intersection of language variations and writing. In terms of research frontiers, the co-occurrence network identifies important research topics, such as "academic writing," "translation," and "bilingualism," which demonstrate a scholarly interest in understanding how these areas interact with trans-practices. These topics might suggest an increasing research focus on more practical applications of trans-theory, particularly within educational and academic contexts. With regard to the interconnectedness of themes, the strength of the links between keywords indicates strong relationships among these topics. For instance, the robust connection between "translanguaging" and "writing" signals an interweaving of these themes in the research, which suggests that scholars are actively exploring how the theory of translanguaging is reflected in and influences writing practices. Similarly, links between "translanguaging" and "literacy" or "biliteracy" point toward a research trend focused on how trans-practices influence literacy development. In summary, the co-occurrence network presents a visual map of the research trends in trans-studies on writing. By exploring the most frequently occurring keywords, their connections, and the strength of these links, we can identify the prevailing themes, emerging research frontiers, and their interconnections within this research area.

3.5 Research Implications

This section presents a bibliometric analysis of trans-studies on writing drawn from Scopus data. The increasing volume of journal articles published on this subject points to an expanding interest in trans-approaches to writing. Within this burgeoning research area, certain journal articles have garnered particular attention. Canagarajah (2011a) and Horner, Lu, Royster, and Trimbur (2011) stand out as the two most frequently cited works. However, it is crucial to highlight that García and Kleifgen's (2020) publication – the only one from the 2020s – has already secured a position among the most frequently cited. Moving forward, our co-occurrence analysis of keywords brought to light five distinct clusters, each representing a specific research topic within trans-studies on writing. Moreover, this analysis unveiled the most frequently employed key-words and their interconnections, which offer insights into the trending focal points and associations within recent trans-scholarship on writing.

The findings from this bibliometric analysis provide insights into the concep-tualization of trans-terms within the academic discourse on writing and, more broadly, language studies. Several pertinent points can be drawn with respect to existing concerns about trans-studies on writing, such as an overemphasis on performance, the flattening of language differences, and the downplaying of language norms and writing conventions. Firstly, the frequent citation of Canagarajah (2011a) and Horner, Lu, Royster, and Trimbur (2011) underscores the substantial impact these works have had on the research area, particularly in shaping the discourse around trans-terms. Both of these works offer nuanced perspectives on the multifaceted nature of language use, emphasizing a performance-centered understanding of language and writing. Their high citation count suggests that their conceptualization of trans-terms, which emphasize fluidity, hybridity, and the dynamic nature of language and writing, has been broadly discussed and has elicited some concerns about the over-emphasis on performance in trans-studies on writing. Future research is needed to address these concerns by investigating trans-practices underlying the visible and audible convergence of semiotic resources.

Secondly, the prominence of keywords such as "translanguaging," "multilin-gualism," and "translation" in the co-occurrence network signals an ongoing engagement with the idea of language difference. Rather than flattening lan-guage differences, these terms suggest an appreciation for the richness of language diversity and the complex ways in which multiple languages interact within the writing process. Nonetheless, future research is necessary to explore how linguistic, social, cultural, historical, educational, and political differences between languages or named languages impact dynamic trans-practices in the writing process. Finally, some critiques have argued that trans-studies may downplay language norms and writing conventions, while the frequent occurrences of keywords such as "academic writing," "literacy," and "L2 writing" imply a continued focus on these aspects within the topic. The persistence of these terms suggests that scholars within trans-studies are not ignoring language norms and conventions but rather are engaging with them in a more critical and nuanced manner. Thus, the results of this bibliometric analysis help respond to the concerns about trans-studies on writing by illustrating the topic's commitment to a nuanced understanding of language use, its recognition of language diversity, and its critical engagement with language norms and conventions. When implementing and researching trans-approaches in writing education, it is essential to consider all these concerns and responses. Doing so will ensure we establish an informed, critical, and inclusive framework that effectively meets various teaching and learning goals.

4 Trans-practices in EAL Writing

In prior sections, we have reviewed the concepts and considerations revolving around trans-terms and reported and discussed the research trends that tackle these aspects. This section delves deeper into trans-practices in EAL writing with a focus on the writing process of two doctoral students, referred to here as Mary and Jake, as they collaborated on a conference proposal. The setting for this investigation is a large public university based in the United States, where Mary and Jake were pursuing their doctorates. They both belonged to the same doctoral cohort, shared Mandarin as their first language, and held degrees in English-related fields. Furthermore, at the time of data collection, they served as first-year composition instructors in their doctoral program. Our focal subjects, Mary and Jake, shared a mutual interest in quantitative studies. They had partnered on a research project focused on data-driven learning (DDL) and stance adverbials – adverbials such as perhaps, clearly, frankly, and sadly that convey the speaker's stance. Their project had been in progress for roughly four months when they decided to submit a proposal for an international academic conference. The combination of their shared research pursuits, collaborative experience, and linguistic backgrounds offered a rich canvas for exploring their language practices and ideologies. Their unique blend of interests and experience provided an invaluable perspective in examining their trans-practices in EAL writing.

The data collection adopted an emic approach, focusing on the participants and their strategies and ideologies surrounding EAL writing. Over three weeks, Mary and Jake undertook the writing process for the conference proposal, which included three face-to-face writing sessions held on sequential Saturday afternoons in the graduate lab of their department. The data collection occurred during these sessions, and each participant separately refined the proposal on weekdays via Google Docs and prepared for the following session. Their shared familiarity with the project and past experience fostered a highly productive and efficient collaboration. Each of these meetings lasted from 25 to 35 minutes and was both video and audio-recorded for subsequent analysis. To complement and validate the data, stimulated recall interviews were conducted immediately following each writing session. As part of these interviews, the participants watched the recorded videos, which enabled them to provide fresh, immediate reflections. These recordings shed light on their language performance, while the stimulated recall interviews offered a window into their language ideologies. These interviews were audio recorded. Their interaction during the writing sessions involved a blend of Mandarin and English. The stimulated recall interviews were purposely conducted in English to gauge their language proficiency and explore how they employed language resources across different contexts, audiences, and purposes. The drafts of their conference proposal, produced across the three writing sessions, were also collected. The accumulated data were sorted into three categories: (1) textual documents, encompassing the three drafts of their conference proposal; (2) video recordings, containing the three recorded writing sessions; and (3) audio recordings, comprising six audio files from the stimulated recall interviews.

In this study, we employed Multimodal Conversation Analysis (MCA) (Tai & Wong, 2023) to analyze the video data and discern the trans-practices of the two students. Multimodal Conversation Analysis, according to Brouwer and Wagner (2004), "focuses on how social order is co-constructed by the members of a social group" and "discusses the ways in which people live and act in the world." (p. 30). Additionally, Tai and Li (2021) described it as a method that delivers a "fine-grained analysis of the social interaction" (p. 613). The data transcription followed the conventions set by Ochs, Schegloff, and Thompson (1996) and Nishino and Atkinson (2015). Through MCA, we evaluated the problem-solving sequences of the participants (such as when they revised the conference proposal's title) within their particular, dynamic writing contexts. This approach helped uncover how language and other semiotic resources were synergistically utilized and situated in the negotiation and construction of meaning. Analyzing the dynamic and complex interactions between the participants allowed for a deeper understanding of the trans-practices used in and for EAL writing. In conjunction with MCA, qualitative thematic analysis (Braun & Clarke, 2006) was employed to investigate the participants' perceptions of their trans-practices during the EAL writing process. To ensure a consistent, coherent, and rigorous analysis, we applied a dual-method approach: deductive coding and inductive coding. Deductive coding was based on the participants' trans-practices and ideologies, while inductive coding followed emerging themes from the data sets. The analysis process started with deductive coding; during this stage, we familiarized ourselves with the complete data set – watching and transcribing video recordings, listening to and transcribing interviews, reading the participants' written drafts, and taking extensive notes. We then embarked on inductive coding, guided by the themes that surfaced from the three data sets. Following this process, we identified two primary themes: EAL writing strategies (inclusive of linguistic and other semiotic strategies) and ideologies (encompassing adapting to academic contexts, challenging monolingual orientations, and situating in rhetorical situations). We continually reviewed and refined these themes and subthemes to ensure the reliability of our results. Notably, while the participants consented to using video content, audio data, and written products, they did not permit using their video images. Therefore, we did not include any video images in this section.

4.1 Trans-strategies in EAL Writing Practices

Throughout their EAL writing process, both doctoral students used various linguistic and semiotic resources to foster negotiation and construct meaning. In the following, we interpret their use of these resources as strategic maneuvers in both linguistic and semiotic domains.

Linguistic strategies, in this context, refer to the students' use of different language resources to fulfill their rhetorical objectives throughout the EAL writing process. The gathered data revealed that the students integrated different language resources (e.g., Mandarin and English) in their oral discussions while limiting their written output (the three drafts) exclusively to English form throughout the EAL writing process. This strategic deployment of language resources in distinct rhetorical situations exemplified their linguistic strategies. Specifically, they challenged monolingualism by crafting a unique language blend in their spoken communication while aligning with broader academic norms by adhering to English language norms and writing conventions in their written work. Their first linguistic strategy, challenging monolingualism, was evident in their conversations. They merged Mandarin and English while deliberating how to adjust the title of their proposal to better align with the objectives and requisites of the intended conference, as showcased in Excerpt 1.

Excerpt 1 (M refers to Mary; J refers to Jake; words and sentences in parentheses were our translation)

M: 首先, 如果我们要往 *AACL* 投的话 *(First, if we submit it to 'AACL')*

J: 嗯 *(Right)*

M: 那肯定是以 *corpus* 为主, 对吗?

　(It has to be based on the 'corpus', right?)

J: 嗯 *(Right)*

M: 所以, 你先看看这两个点, 什么叫做 *stance adverbials*? 什么叫 *DDL*?

　(So, you look at these two points first, what is 'stance adverbials'? what is 'DDL'?)

J: 嗯 *(Right)*

M: 对吧? *(Right?)*

J: 嗯, 反正我觉得可能 *AACL*, 那个会更偏方法论一点

(Right, anyway I think 'AACL' might focus more on methodology)

M: 对 *(Right)*

J: 然后像这种 *pedagogical* 这种*implication*

(Then like this kind of 'pedagogical', this kind of 'implication')

M: *implication* 可以少讲 *(Can talk less about 'implication')*

J: 所以说是不是这个 *title* 要稍微*fix*一下?

(So, does the 'title' need to be slightly 'fixed'?)

M: 我觉得没有必要问什么 *teachers teach* 不 *teach* 或者 *students learn* 不 learn

　(I think it is not necessary to ask 'teachers teach' don't 'teach' or 'students learn'

　don't 'learn')

J: 对 *(Right)*

Excerpt 1 features the students' attempt to revise the title of their proposal based on their decision to submit it to the *American Association of Corpus Linguistics* (AACL). Mary proposed, "首先, 如果我们要往 AACL 投的话 " (First, if we submit it to AACL), "那肯定是以 corpus 为主, 对吗?" (It has to be based on the corpus, right?), to which Jake responded, "所以说是不是这个 title 要稍微 fix 一下?" (So, does the title need to be slightly fixed?). These linguistic expressions from the conversation between the two doctoral students exemplified the agency of language users in shaping their own language. Importantly, it highlights their challenge to the monolingual approach traditionally adopted in the writing process, that is, one language at a time.

The second linguistic strategy manifested prominently in the three drafts of the two students' proposal. Given the academic context where English dominates, they opted to utilize English exclusively. This decision took into account the fact that the AACL conference primarily took place in US universities and required proposals to be written in English. For instance, their initial draft was structured with bullet points, populated exclusively by English words and phrases, as demonstrated in the following bullet points:

- DDL [Data Driven Learning] advantages & inductive vs deductive
- Research design: 1 2 3 (details: 50 mins → participants)
- ENG 106i → **argumentative**, interview, proposal, synthesis (emphasis and color in original)

They developed these English words and phrases into paragraphs in their second draft. For instance, they started their second draft with the following sentences:

> As the fast development of technology in 1990s, corpora began to be integrated in the context of the second language education. Influenced by this trend, data-driven learning (DDL), has receives increasing attention.

These sentences were revised and edited in their third draft as the following (the revised parts were in bold):

> The fast development of **computerized corpora has helped their integration into** the context of second language education. Influenced by this trend, data-driven learning (DDL), has **received** increasing attention. (emphasis added).

Despite employing their distinct language (i.e., the meshing of different language resources) for oral communication, the two doctoral students conformed to English writing norms in their proposal development. They made revisions to align their sentences with English syntax. For instance, they refined "integrated in" and "has receives" to "integration into" and "has received," respectively, to be "grammatically correct." These adjustments indicate not only a keen adherence to English grammar but also a dedication to upholding appropriate academic writing conventions. An example of the latter is their substitution of the general term "technology" with the more specific "computerized corpora," which helped to enhance the precision and focus of their writing.

Creating meaningful discourse extends beyond mere language usage; it incorporates a multitude of semiotic elements. This was evident in the EAL writing process of the two students, who employed semiotic strategies to support their writing. These strategies encompassed various visual components, such as gestures, facial expressions, and eye contact, all of which were used to augment their communicative effectiveness. The collected data demonstrated their use of different semiotic resources in their oral and written communication. For example, during their oral interactions, they melded nonverbal cues with language to deliver their intended meanings efficiently. To substantiate this, we draw attention to Excerpt 1 again, where examples of deployed semiotic resources are highlighted in bold.

Excerpt 1

M: ((puts right hand on her forehead with a thinking face as Jake is reading the title)) 首先,
如果我们要往 *AACL* ((**writes the four letters with right hand fingers in the air**)) 的话
(First, if we submit it to 'AACL')
J: 嗯 *(Right)*
M: 那肯定是以 *corpus* 为主 ((**points with right hand-fingers**)),
对吗?
(It has to be based on the 'corpus', right?)
. . .
J: 所以说 ((**move body slightly forward**)) 是不是这个 *title* 要
稍微 *fix* 一下? ((**sits straight up with smile on his face**)) (*So, does the 'title' need to be slightly 'fixed'?*)
M: 我觉得 ((**looks back**)) 没有必要问什 ((**turns her face toward Jake and looks up and left at Jake's eyes**)) *teachers teach* 不 *teach* ((**moves eyes back**)) 或者 *students learn* 不 *learn*
(I think it is not necessary to ask 'teachers teach' don't 'teach' or 'students learn' don't 'learn')
J: 对 ((**taps lightly with his fingers**)) *(Right)*

Just before Mary said, "首先, 如果我们要往 AACL 投的话" (First, if we submit it to AACL), she placed her right hand on her forehead with a "thinking face." As expounded by Nishino and Atkinson (2015), such a thinking face serves dual purposes – it is both a manifestation of personal cognition and a socially functional visible indicator of thought. Mary's thoughtful countenance, in conjunction with her spoken words, emphasized her dedication to revising the proposal title. Similarly, as Jake said, "所以说, 是不是这个 title 要稍微 fix 一下?" (So, does the 'title' need to be slightly 'fixed'?), he subtly leaned forward, sat upright, and wore a smile on his face. Through these physical gestures – leaning in and maintaining an upright posture – he relayed his eagerness to contribute intellectually to the problem-solving process. Additionally, his polite smile facilitated a questioning tone and a call for suggestions, thus fostering smoother communication. The employment of semiotic resources in their oral interactions played a crucial role in sustaining their conversations, thereby effectively facilitating the realization of their communicative goals.

The proposal drafting process employs a different set of resources for conveying meaning compared to oral communication. Within their three drafts, the two students exploited various textual features such as fonts, colors, and sizes to augment their message delivery. For example, they selected the Calibri font of size 11, applied the color red, and utilized bullet points, arrows, and bolded text to underscore and elaborate their ideas, as demonstrated in the following sentences.

- DDL [Data Driven Learning] advantages & inductive vs deductive
- Research design: 1 2 3 (details: 50 mins → participants)
- ENG 106i → **argumentative**, interview, proposal, synthesis (emphasis and color in original)

To enhance their EAL writing, the students amalgamated semiotic resources (including languages) by deploying some strategic techniques, such as adopting a legible font and size for easy reading, highlighting areas in red that required further scrutiny, structuring their thoughts via bullet points, and indicating logical links with arrows. However, in their second draft, they reconsidered these visual aids and decided to use consistent font and size. This change indicated their increased cognizance of academic EAL writing conventions, such as clarity, coherence, and cohesion, as exemplified in the following sentences.

> As the fast development of technology in 1990s, corpora began to be integrated in the context of the second language education. Influenced by this trend, data-driven learning (DDL), has receives increasing attention.

In their final draft, they modified the font and size. Specifically, they transitioned from Calibri of size 11 to Times New Roman of size 12, a change that aligns with established academic styles such as APA and MLA, as depicted in the following sentences.

> The fast development of computerized corpora has helped their integration into the context of second language education. Influenced by this trend, data-driven learning (DDL), has received increasing attention.

The synergy of these linguistic and semiotic resources facilitated the construction and negotiation of meaning in the students' EAL writing process. This highlights their implementation of trans-strategies, including linguistic and semiotic ones, employed to comprehend and enhance their EAL writing.

4.2 Language Ideologies in Trans-writing Practices

The integration of linguistic and semiotic resources in the EAL writing process of the two students can be viewed as trans-practices. Their demonstrated applications of these resources across varied rhetorical scenarios offer insight into their language ideologies. These include accommodating academic contexts, challenging monolingual norms, and adapting to the nuances of different rhetorical situations.

The findings reveal that the two students opted to conform to established English language norms and writing conventions to succeed in academia. As disclosed by their experiences, they adhered to these strategies primarily due to concerns about the possible repercussions of failing to do so, which might include audience confusion, proposal rejection, or ineffective communication. Mary provided a specific example illustrating this.

> we have to consider the feelings of the listeners. It's really difficult, well if I am a listener who doesn't know Mandarin, I will have a difficult time. If the listener is Japanese, I would keep the English only because if I just mix Chinese or something, it would just confuse people, right?

Jake shared a similar idea and explained that he wrote this research proposal for an academic conference in the United States. To ensure clear communication in this context, he "was comfortable using English" to avoid any potential confusion or inefficiency.

The two students' learning experiences significantly influenced their language practices. Mary articulated that "we came up with these corpus linguistics terms entirely in English. When we came to the field, it was entirely in English. ... I learn all the statistics here in States. ... so, it would be easier for us to communicate in English terms." Jake added that his education in statistics and corpus terms was in English, and he was "not sure whether Chinese linguists use the Chinese terms the same way we use the corresponding English terms, so it is easier to use English terms to avoid misunderstandings." Therefore, they both asserted a preference and comfort in adhering to English language norms and writing conventions within academic contexts. Jake further expressed, "I have been in the U.S. for six years. So, I get used to writing something in English. If you want me to write something in Chinese, it's gonna be in social contexts, and for academic contexts, I just use English." Mary echoed a similar sentiment, stating, "In an academic aspect, most of the academic vocabulary I learn is in English in the first place. For Chinese, probably, more daily-life related." These findings demonstrated that these two students tailored their academic writing approach based on their beliefs about using different language resources, such as English and Mandarin, for various situations, such as academic versus social contexts, and their concerns regarding the mixing of languages, such as codemeshing.

Mary and Jake's EAL writing approach highlighted their tendency to blend language resources, regardless of their preference for English in academic contexts. This practice emerged from their shared identities as Mandarin-speaking Chinese individuals, fellow doctoral students, and collaborative researchers with overlapping interests. They reasoned that this blend of language resources facilitated their communication efficiency and enhanced their ability to negotiate meaning. Jake, for instance, remarked that "there are two Chinese people, and there is no point in communicating with each other in English only. Both of us communicate efficiently [in Mandarin and English]." Mary also stated, "it [using both Mandarin and English to communicate with another Mandarin speaker who shares a similar background] is more straightforward, and it's just so weird that two Chinese are talking in English only." Additionally, Mary and Jake noted their shared academic journey, which was being second-year doctoral students at a U.S. university. They attended certain courses together, including those in their major and statistical courses, due to their shared research interest in the quantitative approach to language studies. Thus, they were comfortable blending language resources during their exchanges.

Furthermore, both students actively resisted monolingual perspectives to pursue their rhetorical goals more effectively. Jake expressed that "[communicating in both Mandarin and English] definitely releases the cognitive burden in my mind. We have the competence to communicate in English and Mandarin [respectively], but we have to process, you know, the language in our mind at the same time we process the content, so we just release the language burden from our mind and focus on the content." Mary agreed and said that "it's easier to communicate in both languages." In discussing their choice of language resources for communication, both agreed on the practice of blending English terms, concepts, and other relevant knowledge acquired through English instruction with Mandarin. The reason was that they were unfamiliar with the Mandarin equivalents of these English terms or concepts and found it simpler and more efficient to use English terms directly instead of translating those terms into Mandarin. This meshing of English and Mandarin proved to be more effective and efficient for constructing and negotiating meaning. Their demonstrated strategies did not align with the discrete ideologies of monolingualism and translingualism. Instead, their ideologies were interwoven and negotiated based on fluid rhetorical situations.

These ideologies suggest that Mary and Jake adhered to English writing norms and conventions for academic text creation while concurrently challenging monolingual norms to attain communicative objectives. However, they transcended this binary approach by balancing accommodation and resistance and situating themselves in dynamic rhetorical situations. Mary and Jake elaborated that their strategies were tailored to their specific objectives, audiences, and situations. In particular, they were drafting a research proposal for an academic conference and conversing in person, which allowed them to focus solely on each other without considering other audiences with diverse backgrounds, objectives, and contexts. This afforded them the ability to construct meaning more deliberately and confidently. For instance, Jake stated, "I think we [Mary and Jake] just do code-switching, and that makes us comfortable. We don't really worry about using English words or Chinese words, just naturally say something." Mary added, "I do it [meshing Mandarin and English to make meaning] naturally, especially in this multilingual and multicultural context." Their language usage could be construed as trans-practices, although they presented their trans-voices in English form in their written works to align with potential audience expectations. Hence, the English form in their text can be considered translingual English (Dovchin, 2021; Dvochin & Dryden, 2022) in that the Mandarin used in their oral exchanges played a role in shaping their written text. They both recognized that their written work's audience would be conference proposal reviewers, and the goal of the proposal was to demonstrate the potential and significance of their research and persuade the reviewers to accept their proposal. Despite different audiences, purposes, and contexts leading to the adherence to EAL writing norms and conventions in their written products, the voices conveyed in the text were translingual. In this respect, they both accommodated and resisted English academic norms and writing conventions to position themselves and their writing within fluid rhetorical situations.

4.3 EAL Writing beyond Boundaries

This study's findings highlight the need to move beyond a focus on linguistic features and language proficiency when examining EAL writing. Instead, they underline the importance of understanding EAL writing as trans-practices, where writers engage in a complex situation with their potential or envisaged audiences by navigating linguistic, cultural, and semiotic resources, norms, and conventions. Shifting from structuralist orientations to a perspective of trans-practices, as suggested by Canagarajah (2018), can empower multilingual writers by providing them with space to draw from their full linguistic repertoire to foster inclusivity of deviations from linguistic norms and writing conventions. It is crucial to understand that embracing a trans-perspective does not equate disregarding or opposing English norms and writing conventions.

Instead, this study's findings propose viewing these norms and conventions as valuable resources at the disposal of writers. By embracing these norms and conventions, multilingual writers can enhance their linguistic repertoire, promote their agency, deepen their understanding of their trans-practices, and effectively position their writing within the broader academic context. Echoing previous studies (Kim & Chang, 2022; Ollerhead et al., 2020), acknowledging EAL writing as trans-practices can be beneficial for both educators and learners as this recognition appreciates the complex nature of EAL writing and fosters an inclusive educational environment. However, it is equally essential to recognize the significant role English language norms and writing conventions play in EAL writing. Accepting these norms allows multilingual writers to meet academic expectations while effectively engaging in trans-practices and utilizing their unique linguistic and cultural resources.

The essence of EAL writing as trans-practices necessitates a process-oriented perspective. It is paramount to understand that trans-practices should not be reduced solely to the act of codemeshing. Our findings illustrate that while the written output of the two students was in English form and may not fall under the codemeshing category, the voices that resonated within the text were inherently translingual. This translingual essence was born from the construction and negotiation of meaning using an array of linguistic and semiotic resources. These findings echo Schreiber and Watson's (2018) response to Gevers (2018), which emphasized that trans-practices are broader than codemeshing and codemeshing is a matter of agency in trans-practices. Furthermore, our findings endorse Guerra (2016) and Lu and Horner (2016), who advocated for the interpretation of trans-practices from a rhetorical perspective rather than through product-oriented codemeshing. Gilyard (2016) also argued that rhetorical astuteness is more important than mimicking any specific strategy, such as codemeshing. These insights suggest that trans-practices should not be limited to any particular form of writing. Instead, they should be seen as rhetorical instruments that enrich and propel EAL writing in the writing process. The fluidity, negotiability, and permeability of boundaries tied to language, language difference, and language use should be recognized and understood. Acknowledging these elements can help multilingual writers to better understand trans-practices and improve their EAL writing while navigating and surpassing traditional linguistic and cultural barriers.

The fluid rhetorical situations in which writers operate serve as the foundation for understanding their trans-practices. The EAL writing process of the two doctoral students examined in this study serves as an illustration of how trans-practices can adapt to various contexts, audiences, and purposes. Their distinct strategies in response to these dynamic rhetorical situations underscored the fluid nature of trans-practices in their writing process. These insights highlight the value of adopting a trans-perspective in the examination of EAL writing. It allows a comprehensive analysis of how multilingual writers engage with a diverse set of resources within these dynamic rhetorical situations. Such a view can enrich our comprehension of EAL writing by acknowledging multilingual writers' fluid interactions with various resources for different rhetorical goals. These findings are in tune with the argument that student writers need to cultivate a rhetorical sensibility that perceives language as an emergent, adaptive practice rather than a fixed, standardized construct (Guerra, 2016). As Bou Ayash (2016) posited, educators play a critical role in guiding students to comprehend and employ their trans-practices with this rhetorical sensibility. To cultivate a rhetorical sensibility, multilingual writers must initially understand language norms and writing conventions (Canagarajah, 2018), such as how they are established and why they are ever-evolving. In other words, before they can challenge or resist them, multilingual writers need to understand them and recognize that they are negotiable and fluid. The two students' production of English text to articulate trans-voices reinforces the necessity to consider language norms and writing conventions when examining trans-practices from a rhetorical perspective. These norms and conventions have a significant impact on the shaping of voice and should not be dismissed lightly. By embracing a trans-approach and acknowledging the role of language norms and writing conventions, we can deepen our understanding of the language practices of multilingual writers and foster their rhetorical growth in EAL writing.

4.4 Summary

This study illuminates the need to perceive EAL writing as trans-practices to bridge linguistic and cultural boundaries. The findings reinforce the interwoven relationships between writers, their intended audiences, and the linguistic, cultural, and semiotic resources they utilize to construct meaning. By adopting trans-perspective, multilingual writers are empowered to harness their capabilities, cultivate agency, and be inclusive of deviations from linguistic and cultural norms. It is crucial to underscore that trans-practices extend beyond codemeshing. This is evidenced by the writings of the two doctoral students: although their texts appeared to be in English form, they integrated diverse linguistic, cultural, and semiotic resources in the writing process, thereby reflecting trans-voices. This finding resonates with a rhetorical approach to trans-practices, which argues that fostering rhetorical awareness and recognizing language as a contingent, dynamic practice should be prioritized over mimicking codemeshing. This rhetorical approach encourages multilingual writers to familiarize themselves with language norms and writing conventions and acknowledge their fluidity and negotiability. With this comprehension of norms and conventions in trans-practices, writers are better equipped to navigate and interact with them effectively in and for different rhetorical situations. The language strategies of the two doctoral students exemplify the dynamism of trans-practices within fluid rhetorical situations. Acknowledging this fluidity enables a comprehensive examination of how multilingual writers employ diverse resources and rhetorical sensibility in their EAL writing. Therefore, educators play a pivotal role in steering students toward developing this rhetorical sensibility to broaden their repertoire, enhance their agency and creativity, and situate their writing within the broader academic contexts.

5 Implications of Trans-pedagogies for EAL Writing

The blossoming of trans-approaches in writing studies – encompassing theoretical and practical facets – has given rise to promising trans-pedagogies in EAL writing education. Nevertheless, the enactment of these trans-pedagogies has elicited scholarly debates within the trans-academic community and between trans- and L2 writing scholars, highlighting the benefits and challenges these pedagogies bring. Recent research (Cavazos, 2017; Kim & Chang, 2022) has exemplified the efficacy of trans-pedagogies. Their findings suggest that trans-approaches can heighten rhetorical sensibility, treat non-English language resources as assets, foster inclusive and open educational environments, and augment metalinguistic awareness among students. However, there are also challenges, including the continued dominance of English monolingualism, the contentious issue of codemeshing, insufficient guidance for teachers and students in their trans-practices, and the potential for the marginalization of students from linguistically minoritized backgrounds (Kafle, 2020; Kuteeva, 2020; Sun, 2022, 2023). These findings indicate the need to incorporate trans-pedagogies into EAL writing instruction while adapting them to suit specific rhetorical situations and preparing both educators and learners for their implementation. Furthermore, it is essential to address relevant concerns to mitigate the risk of biased implementation. Therefore, this section will delve into the implications of trans-pedagogies for EAL writing.

5.1 Complementing rather than Replacing Currently Practiced EAL Writing Pedagogies

Trans-pedagogies introduce new dimensions to EAL writing education, yet they should not be perceived as a replacement but rather a complement to established EAL writing pedagogies. This perspective is rooted in the necessity to accommodate the broad spectrum of needs present in EAL classrooms. For instance,

Bou Ayash (2016) found variances in students' responses to trans-practices, with some EAL learners eager to contest monolingual ideologies while others experienced anxiety around incorporating non-English resources in high-stakes writing situations. Similarly, from the educators' perspective, Arnold's (2016) research unveiled a mixed response, with some EAL teachers embracing a trans-approach as a means to challenge monolingualism and leverage students' linguistic and cultural resources for learning while others worried about adequately preparing their students for academic success through this approach. These findings underscore the assertion that EAL learners' needs are diverse, and thus, a uniform writing pedagogy will not fit all. To effectively cater to this diverse need, it is vital for EAL writing teachers to consider an amalgamation of trans-pedagogies with other instructional approaches, such as EAP, genre, and sociocultural ones. In support of this, Du et al. (2020) proposed a fusion of trans-principles within an EAP curriculum to aid students in adapting their writing skills to various rhetorical situations. Similarly, Sun and Zhang (2022) recommended the integration of trans-pedagogies with digital feedback to help students experiment with language use and refine their writing abilities. These cases illustrate the potential to adjust trans-pedagogies to suit students' unique needs, as opposed to utilizing them as a standalone method. In short, EAL writing instructors should acknowledge the varied learning needs of their students and thoughtfully craft their pedagogies – potentially an amalgamation of trans- and other approaches – based on diverse rhetorical situations to foster a more inclusive and effective learning environment.

Another reason for trans-pedagogies to complement rather than replace existing EAL writing pedagogies is the documented efficacy of the latter. A number of current EAL writing pedagogies, including process (Lam, 2015; Zamel, 1983), genre (Hyland, 2007; Worden, 2018), and corpus (Lan et al., 2022; Lu, 2017), have consistently been demonstrated as effective in enhancing students' writing skills. For example, Lam's (2015) study found that the process writing approach, which encourages EAL students to negotiate meaning and engages them in the writing process, can result in improved writing outcomes. Likewise, corpus-based approaches (e.g., Lan et al., 2022) provide a data-driven method to assist EAL students in enhancing their writing skills and improving their writing quality. Genre-based writing (Worden, 2018) has also been evidenced to equip L2 writing teachers and students with a deeper understanding of genre conventions and rhetorical moves. These findings suggest that merging trans-pedagogies with existing EAL writing pedagogies could forge a more comprehensive teaching approach for EAL writing. Trans-pedagogies, with their emphasis on the interconnectedness of language, culture, and power, strive to foster more equitable and inclusive learning environments for EAL students.

Therefore, integrating a trans-perspective with existing EAL writing pedagogies can potentially lead to improved writing outcomes. For instance, incorporating trans-pedagogy in the social dimensions of writing can enlighten students on how their cultural and linguistic backgrounds influence their writing practices in a specific social context, thereby enriching their understanding of the writing process and negotiation of meaning. This infusion of trans-pedagogies into existing EAL writing pedagogies, thus, can contribute to a more equitable and inclusive learning environment and enhance engagement and motivation among EAL students.

Furthermore, the amalgamation of trans-pedagogies and other writing pedagogies can help address the challenges typically associated with trans-concepts. A prominent challenge is the perception of trans-practices as codemeshing (Kafle, 2020; Schreiber & Watson, 2018), which may inadvertently marginalize some linguistically minoritized students (Kuteeva, 2020). However, this concern can be alleviated by integrating trans-pedagogies with other writing pedagogies that emphasize a process-based approach. A study by Llanes and Cots (2022) provided an example by showcasing how a trans-approach, combined with syntactic-complexity research in EAL writing instruction, elevated the metalinguistic awareness and communicative abilities of trans-group students compared to a monolingual group. Pedagogically, this study demonstrated that trans-pedagogies could be integrated with other approaches to enhance EAL writing instruction and help avoid categorizing trans-practices in writing as merely codemeshing. Other research indicates that the integration of trans- and other pedagogies can assist students in honing crucial skills for academic writing success. For instance, integrating trans-pedagogies with Content and Language Integrated Learning (CLIL) has been found beneficial in engaging students in higher-order thinking skills and expressing meanings with diverse language resources in EAL learning (Llinares & Evnitskaya, 2021). The fusion of CLIL and trans-pedagogies has proven to foster a better understanding of academic genres, language usage, and the writing process (Rafi & Morgan, 2023; Xie & Sun, 2023). Another study by Smith et al. (2017) revealed that integrating trans-pedagogies with multimodal pedagogies could enhance students' multimodal literacy skills and boost their writing engagement. These findings advocate for a more comprehensive approach to EAL writing education, which addresses a broad range of writing aspects such as genre, language use, multimodality, and the writing process. The integration of trans- and other writing pedagogies can heighten EAL writing practitioners' understanding that trans-practices do not equate to codemeshing. While the written product may be perceived as "monolingual" (English, e.g.), the writing process remains trans-oriented. Thus, EAL writing teachers should contemplate integrating trans-pedagogies with other writing pedagogies to create a more encompassing approach to EAL writing education. This integration can empower students to navigate their trans-practices more effectively.

5.2 Resisting Monolingualism rather than Language Norms and Writing Conventions

Effectively countering monolingualism with trans-pedagogies in EAL writing education necessitates a deep understanding of what monolingualism entails and its influence on language instruction and learning. Bou Ayash (2016) perceived monolingualism as a language ideology that

> propagates representations of language as fixed, self-standing, having status outside the cultural, political, and economic forces that bring about its practice, ... In composition, its tenets construct a particular variety of English, namely Standard Written English (SWE), as a discrete, invariant, and pre-given hermetically sealed system, the attainment and mastery of which putatively secures social and economic advancement. In doing so, monolingualism attributes agency and intrinsic, perpetual value to the language itself rather than its users/ learners. According to this ideology, the aim of language and literacy instruction is transmitting ostensibly fixed, universal conventions and practices of reading and writing with a valuation of native-like fluency and correctness in reproducing these. In the name of preserving these ideals, any signs of difference or lack of conformity are treated as language deficits to be eradicated. (p. 557)

This perspective frames language as a stable entity, thereby overshadowing the fluid and dynamic nature of language use. The propagation of SWE as the ideal form of EAL writing and the insistence on native-like fluency and correctness perpetuate the belief in a singular "correct" use of English, which marginalizes and negates the linguistic and cultural diversity of multilingual learners. Research has demonstrated that multilingual learners face a myriad of challenges when pressured to comply with SWE norms in academic writing. For instance, Arnold (2020) argued that the pressure to conform to SWE could cause students to lose their unique voice and identity in their writing and drive them to suppress their cultural and linguistic backgrounds to assimilate with the dominant discourse. In addition, the emphasis on native-like fluency and correctness privileges certain forms of English, which can create a linguistic hierarchy that marginalizes speakers of non-standard varieties (Horner, Lu, et al., 2011). Therefore, the advocacy for SWE as the ideal form of EAL writing amplifies linguistic discrimination (Dovchin & Dryden, 2022) and transmits a damaging message to students that their language and culture are inferior to the dominant norms (Barbour & Lickorish Quinn, 2020).

Trans-pedagogies need to discern between endorsing language norms and writing conventions and propagating a monolingual ideology that encourages a single, dominant language at the expense of linguistic and cultural diversity. Language norms and writing conventions, which have developed over time, are pivotal for effective communication. They offer, to a certain extent, a collective comprehension and uniformity in language usage that simplifies communication and understanding. Hence, it is important for trans-pedagogies to oppose monolingualism, not language norms or writing conventions. This involves appreciating the wide array of language and cultural practices and recognizing that there are numerous legitimate ways of utilizing language. In this sense, language norms and writing conventions can be employed to broaden and diversify multilingual learners' linguistic repertoire rather than restricting them to a narrow, standardized version of English. For instance, educators like Kim and Park (2020) and Seltzer (2020) have exposed students to a spectrum of languages, language varieties, and styles and encouraged them to experiment with various forms of expression instead of merely teaching them to adhere to SWE norms. By focusing resistance on monolingualism, not language norms and writing conventions, students can develop a more sophisticated understanding of the cultural and social facets of language. Additionally, it nurtures a sense of pride and ownership in their own linguistic and cultural practices. Nevertheless, it is essential to approach language norms and writing conventions with a critical eye by treating them as fluid, synergistic, and negotiable constructs rather than fixed, discrete, and monolithic entities. In other words, while language norms and writing conventions play a vital role in effective communication, they do not equate to monolingualism. It is crucial for trans-pedagogies to resist monolingualism in order to acknowledge, value, and celebrate linguistic and cultural diversity and to broaden and diversify multilingual learners' linguistic repertoire by critically and creatively using language norms and writing conventions.

Resisting monolingualism rather than language norms and writing conventions enables trans-pedagogies to create a more equitable, open, and inclusive learning environment. This is particularly important for marginalized students who do not share the majority's local languages. By valuing and recognizing the linguistic and cultural diversity of multilingual learners, teachers can shift from a monolingual, English-only ideology toward a more inclusive and respectful approach to language and literacy education (Horner et al., 2010). This is especially critical in contexts where a dominant language is not the mother tongue of all students. Consider, for instance, the English-speaking countries where substantial multilingual populations from diverse linguistic and cultural backgrounds exist. These students may face marginalization and discrimination based on their language backgrounds, and they may struggle to access educational and professional opportunities due to the prevailing belief in monolingual English superiority (Dovchin & Dryden, 2022). By resisting monolingualism and valuing all students' linguistic repertoire, EAL writing teachers can cultivate a more inclusive learning environment where every student feels valued and supported. This involves acknowledging that language usage has many effective forms and that language norms and writing conventions are not rigid, prescriptive linguistic entities but rather evolving, useful resources. In this context, teachers can help dismantle traditional barriers that separate multilingual learners from their monolingual counterparts and foster a more collaborative and inclusive learning community. In this way, trans-pedagogies can empower students to use their linguistic repertoire in critical ways rather than simply conforming to a limited, prescribed set of language norms and writing conventions.

5.3 Designing Trans-pedagogies Based on Rhetorical Situations

Employing trans-pedagogies centered around rhetorical situations is crucial for addressing the diverse needs of EAL learners and engaging them actively in the learning process. As suggested by Guerra (2016), crafting trans-pedagogies that consider the linguistic and cultural backgrounds of students can successfully bridge the gap between their existing knowledge and academic discourse expectations. This indicates that teachers should construct trans-pedagogies that take into account students' linguistic backgrounds, cultural insights, and experiences to build upon their existing knowledge, thereby enhancing their ability to acquire new knowledge effectively. By adopting a rhetorical approach, trans-pedagogies can guide EAL writing teachers in formulating learning activities that mirror the interests, experiences, and learning objectives of students. Horner and Lu (2016) similarly advocated a rhetorical approach to trans-pedagogies for establishing an inclusive and equitable classroom environment that values all students' languages, cultures, identities, interests, experiences, and learning aspirations. Such a rhetorical approach to trans-pedagogies underscores the necessity of immersing students in the writing process through an emphasis on rhetorical situations. In this manner, teachers can encourage students to become active players in the writing process by fostering opportunities for collaboration and feedback. This cultivates a supportive learning community that enhances students' critical thinking and writing capabilities. Furthermore, comprehending the rhetorical situation of a given writing task can enable students to effectively convey their ideas to a specific audience, a skill critical for success in academic and professional environments (Ene et al., 2019). Supporting the effectiveness of trans-pedagogies, a case study by Pacheco et al. (2019) showcased how students could engage meaningfully with texts. The study observed a third-grade teacher strategically engaging in trans-practices to co-construct meaning with students by employing diverse language resources, including English, Arabic, and Spanish. Their findings emphasize the importance of nurturing teachers' trans-competence and developing trans-pedagogies anchored in rhetorical situations. By doing so, teachers can aid students in viewing their linguistic and cultural diversity as assets rather than impediments to learning. Collectively, these studies underline how implementing trans-pedagogies centered around rhetorical situations can stimulate EAL writing students to become active participants in the writing process, bridge the gap between diverse student bodies and traditional EAL writing instruction, and lead to effective learning outcomes.

Another reason for implementing trans-pedagogies rooted in rhetorical situations lies in preparing EAL writing students for real-world interactions. With our world growing more interconnected by the day, the ability to effectively communicate across diverse cultures and languages is gaining increasing importance. Trans-pedagogy can equip students with the vital skills and competencies to traverse the diverse and intricate scenarios of real-world communication. For instance, a study by Ene et al. (2019) provided four post-graduate EAL writing students with opportunities to engage with varied texts and concepts. The results indicated that the students' trans-practices shifted based on the rhetorical situations, thereby revealing the necessity of trans-pedagogies in aiding students to develop a more sophisticated understanding of different cultures and perspectives. In this vein, trans-pedagogies can guide students toward a more nuanced comprehension of language and its communication role and foster critical thinking and cultural awareness. This, in turn, can improve motivation, self-esteem, and academic achievement. Further supporting this notion, a mixed-method study by Eren (2022) discovered that trans-awareness significantly predicts intercultural communicative competence, which indicates that individuals with higher trans-awareness are more adept at intercultural communication. Moreover, the study uncovered that certain classroom practices, such as trans-practices, managing intercultural tensions, and incorporating technology into the classroom, could enhance intercultural competence. These findings offer evidence of trans-pedagogies' effectiveness in preparing students for real-world challenges by enhancing their intercultural competence. These studies reveal that the enactment of trans-pedagogies rooted in rhetorical situations can successfully prepare EAL writing students for real-world success by fostering intercultural communication, critical thinking, and cultural awareness. Therefore, trans-pedagogies based on rhetorical situations can facilitate students in acquiring essential skills for academic and professional success, such as tailoring their writing to diverse contexts and audiences.

Implementing trans-pedagogies grounded in rhetorical situations can contribute to promoting social justice within language and communication by equipping students with the ability to identify and confront inequalities and biases. These pedagogical strategies can assist students in cultivating a critical awareness of the inherent power dynamics embedded within language use and communication scenarios. Engaging in the analysis of texts and communication contexts from multiple perspectives allows students to gain a comprehensive understanding of how language can serve as a tool for the empowerment or marginalization of different groups (Lee, 2016). An insightful exploration by Canagarajah and Dovchin (2019) delved into the trans-practices of young individuals from diverse geographic regions, such as Mongolia and Japan, and probed the political implications embedded in their daily language choices and the potential they held for resistance. Their findings highlight how trans-practices can play a critical role in challenging imbalances of power and fostering social justice. Therefore, it is imperative that trans-pedagogies are designed to enable students to acquire the skills necessary to confront inequalities and champion social justice based on specific rhetorical situations. By facilitating opportunities for students to participate in advocacy work or leverage their writing skills to raise awareness about societal issues, EAL writing teachers can empower students to evolve into agents of change within their communities. Such active participation in instigating social change will pave the way toward a more equitable and just society as they prepare to navigate the intricate landscapes of real-world social and communication situations. In a recent study by Zhang-wu and Tian (2023), it was found that trans-pedagogies could enhance students' critical thinking about the role of English in education, academia, and communication for social justice. This progression, in turn, can culminate in more inclusive and equitable communication practices across society. Therefore, the implementation of trans-pedagogies based on rhetorical situations can contribute to fostering social justice in language and communication by empowering students to identify and confront inequities and biases, intensifying their critical awareness of language use power dynamics, and enhancing their adaptability in a range of communication situations.

These implications of trans-pedagogies for EAL writing education suggest that their implementation requires thoughtful, informed, and critical planning. Trans-approaches hold significant potential for challenging established nationalist and neoliberal ideologies, thereby fostering social justice in language education. This necessitates a thorough understanding of how to effectively integrate trans-concepts and pedagogies into various aspects of education, including curriculum development, teaching methods, and language evaluation. Such exploration could lead to teaching practices that are more inclusive and effective, particularly in contexts where English is not the dominant language. These pedagogical practices would acknowledge and utilize the rich linguistic diversity of students. Additionally, a closer examination of the roles of different named languages in trans-practices can offer important insights. Understanding these roles can guide the development of language policies and practices that are more reflective of and responsive to the multilingual realities of students, which can further enhance their educational experiences. Therefore, a balanced approach is essential in trans-oriented EAL writing education. Overemphasis on performance might lead to overlooking crucial aspects such as language competence and historical context, which are critical in academic writing for achieving explicit expression and mutual understanding among diverse audiences. Therefore, it is important to maintain this balance in trans-pedagogies. Moreover, there is a need for more practical, empirically based recommendations on integrating trans-concepts and pedagogies into academic writing. This would not only contribute to a more inclusive academic environment but also prompt a reevaluation of traditional academic discourse norms. Moreover, further empirical research into the dynamics of power relations, social inequality, and the consequences of excessively focusing on performance is increasingly recognized as necessary. Such research aligns with the call for a more holistic and socially conscious approach in language studies, which might help mitigate the intricate challenges in trans-writing studies and beyond.

5.4 Conclusion

This section has discussed the potential of trans-pedagogies in transforming EAL writing education into a more inclusive, equitable, and effective process. By embracing trans-pedagogical methods, teachers can cultivate engaging and productive learning environments that consider the diverse linguistic and cultural backgrounds of EAL students. Such pedagogical approaches stimulate a more collaborative, dialogic, and critical learning style to empower students to articulate their perspectives and ideas with their entire linguistic repertoire. This interactive strategy can enhance students' confidence and motivation, enabling them to uniquely express their thoughts in EAL writing based on their linguistic, sociocultural, and educational backgrounds. Moreover, trans-pedagogies underscore the significance of incorporating different teaching and learning methods to validate different forms of communication and inspire students to employ multiple modalities, languages, and literacies for self-expression. By integrating a variety of media and technologies into their lesson plans, educators can support students in refining their communication skills in a holistic and integrated manner. Ultimately, this reinforces the notion that the purpose of language learning extends beyond simply acquiring a new language – it also involves understanding and appreciating the diversity and richness of different cultures, ideas, and perspectives.

In conclusion, the adoption of trans-pedagogies in EAL writing education has the potential to positively influence students' language development, cultural consciousness, and overall academic success. By embracing a trans-pedagogical approach, teachers can cultivate an inclusive, equitable, and efficient learning environment that promotes critical thinking, creativity, and collaboration. Through dialogue-driven and cooperative methods, teachers can empower students to communicate their thoughts and perspectives using their full linguistic repertoire, thereby enhancing their confidence and motivation. Trans-approaches that utilize multiple modes and language resources legitimate students' various ways of communication based on rhetorical situations, which can further increase their writing skills and quality. For the successful implementation of trans-pedagogies in EAL writing classrooms, it is crucial for teachers to receive adequate training and support. This equips them with the necessary skills to integrate these pedagogical methods into their teaching. Additionally, maintaining an inclusive and culturally responsive learning environment is vital to value the diversity of students' linguistic and cultural backgrounds. However, it is essential to acknowledge potential challenges and limitations, such as resistance from students or teachers who are more comfortable with traditional teaching methods or lack of access to resources or technology needed for multimodal approaches. Therefore, a continual process of reflection and evaluation of the effectiveness of trans-pedagogies in the EAL writing classroom is crucial to inform necessary adaptations and adjustments to best support students' needs. This balance between innovative teaching methods and pragmatic classroom management ensures an evolving, responsive EAL learning environment.

References

Arnold, L. R. (2016). "This is a field that's open, not closed": Multilingual and international writing faculty respond to composition theory. *Composition Studies, 44*(1), 72–88.

Arnold, L. R. (2020). "Now I don't use it at all … It's gone": Monolingual ideology, multilingual students, and (failed) translingual negotiation strategies. *Research in the Teaching of English, 54*(4), 318–341.

Atkinson, D. (Ed.). (2011). *Alternative approaches to second language acquisition.* Oxford: Routledge.

Atkinson, D., and Tardy, C. M. (2018). SLW at the crossroads: Finding a way in the field. *Journal of Second Language Writing, 42*, 86–93. https://doi.org/10.1016/j.jslw.2018.10.011.

Atkinson, D., Churchill, E., Nishino, T., and Okada, H. (2007). Alignment and interaction in a sociocognitive approach to second language acquisition. *Modern Language Journal, 91*(2), 169–188. https://doi.org/10.1111/j.1540-4781.2007.00539.x.

Atkinson, D., Crusan, D., Matsuda, P. K. *et al.* (2015). Clarifying the relationship between L2 writing and translingual writing: An open letter to writing studies editors and organization leaders. *College English, 77*(4), 383–386.

Baker, C. (2001). *Foundations of bilingual education and bilingualism* (3rd ed.). New York: Multilingual Matters.

Barbour, C., and Lickorish Quinn, K. (2020). Los pájaros are feliz and are dreaming about gwiazdy: Facilitating translingual creative writing in the primary classroom. *English in Education, 54*, 6–26. https://doi.org/10.1080/04250494.2019.1703553.

Bawarshi, A. (2016). Beyond the genre fixation: A translingual perspective on genre. *College English, 78*(3), 243–249.

Baynham, M., and Lee, T. (2019). *Translation and translanguaging.* Multilingual Matters: Routledge. https://doi.org/10.4324/9781315158877

Beiler, I. R., and Dewilde, J. (2020). Translation as translingual writing practice in English as an additional language. *The Modern Language Journal, 104*(3), 533–549. https://doi.org/10.1111/modl.12660.

Bou Ayash, N. (2016). Conditions of (im)possibility: Postmonolingual language representations in academic literacies. *College English, 78*(6), 555–577.

Braun, V., and Clarke, V. (2006). Using thematic analysis in psychology. *Qualitative Research in Psychology, 3*, 77–101. http://dx.doi.org/10.1191/1478088706qp063oa.

Brouwer, C. E. and Wagner, J. (2004). Developmental issues in second language conversation. *Journal of Applied Linguistics*, *1*, 29–47. https://doi.org/10.1558/japl.v1.i1.29.

Canagarajah, A. S. (2002). Multilingual writers and the academic community: Towards a critical relationship. *Journal of English for Academic Purposes*, *1* (1), 29–44. https://doi.org/10.1016/s1475-1585(02)00007-3.

Canagarajah, A. S. (2006a). The place of world Englishes in composition: Pluralization continued. *College Composition and Communication*, *57*(4), 586–619.

Canagarajah, A. S. (2006b). Toward a writing pedagogy of shuttling between languages: Learning from multilingual writers. *College English*, *68*(6), 589–604. https://doi.org/10.2307/25472177.

Canagarajah, A. S. (2007). Lingua Franca English, multilingual communities, and language acquisition. *Modern Language Journal*, *91*(5), 923–939. https://doi.org/10.1111/j.1540-4781.2007.00678.x.

Canagarajah, A. S. (2009). Multilingual strategies of negotiating English: From conversation to writing. *Journal of Composition Theory*, *29*(1/2), 17–48.

Canagarajah, A. S. (2011a). Codemeshing in academic writing: Identifying teachable strategies of translanguaging. *Modern Language Journal*, *95*(3), 401–417. https://doi.org/10.1111/j.1540-4781.2011.01207.x.

Canagarajah, A. S. (2011b). Translanguaging in the classroom: Emerging issues for research and pedagogy. *Applied Linguistics Review*, *2*, 1–28. https://doi.org/10.1515/9783110239331.1.

Canagarajah, A. S. (2013a). *Translingual practice: Global Englishes and cosmopolitan relations*. Abingdon: Routledge. https://doi.org/10.4324/9780203073889.

Canagarajah, A. S. (2013b). Negotiating translingual literacy: An enactment. *Research in the Teaching of English*, *48*(1), 40–67.

Canagarajah, A. S. (2015). Clarifying the relationship between translingual practice and L2 writing. *Applied Linguistics Review*, *6*(4), 414–440. https://doi.org/10.1515/applirev-2015-0020.

Canagarajah, A. S. (2016). Translingual writing and teacher development in composition. *College English*, *78*(3), 265–273.

Canagarajah, A. S. (2017). *Translingual practices and neoliberal policies: Attitudes and strategies of African skilled migrants in Anglophone workplaces*. Cham: SpringerBriefs in Linguistics. https://doi.org/10.1007/978-3-319-41243-6_1.

Canagarajah, A. S. (2018). Translingual practice as spatial repertoires: Expanding the paradigm beyond structuralist orientations. *Applied Linguistics*, *39*(1), 31–54. https://doi.org/10.1093/applin/amx041.

Canagarajah, A. S. (2022). Challenges in decolonizing linguistics: The politics of enregisterment and the divergent uptakes of translingualism. *Educational Linguistics*, *1*(1), 25–55. https://doi.org/10.1515/eduling-2021-0005.

Canagarajah, A. S. (2023). A decolonial Crip Linguistics. *Applied Linguistics*. https://doi.org/10.1093/applin/amac042.

Canagarajah, A. S., and Dovchin, S. (2019). The everyday politics of translingualism as a resistant practice. *International Journal of Multilingualism*, *16*(2), 127–144. https://doi.org/10.1080/14790718.2019.1575833.

Carson, J., and Leki, I. (Eds.). (1993). *Reading in the composition classroom: Second language perspectives*. Boston, MA: Heinle and Heinle. https://doi.org/10.1017/s027226310001336x.

Cavazos, A. G. (2017). Translingual oral and written practices: Rhetorical resources in multilingual writers' discourses. *International Journal of Bilingualism*, *21*(4), 385–401. https://doi.org/10.1177/1367006916629225.

Cenoz, J., and Gorter, D. (2017). Minority languages and sustainable translanguaging: Threat or opportunity? *Journal of Multilingual and Multicultural Development*, *38*(10), 901–912. https://doi.org/10.1080/01434632.2017.1284855.

Cinaglia, C., and De Costa, P. I. (2022). Cultivating critical translingual awareness: Challenges and possibilities for teachers and teacher educators. *RELC Journal*, *53*(2), 452–459. https://doi.org/10.1177/00336882221113659.

Conference on College Composition and Communication. (1974). "Students" right to their own language [Special issue]. *College Composition and Communication*, 25. https://cdn.ncte.org/nctefiles/groups/cccc/newsrtol.pdf.

Cook, V. (2016). Premises of multi-competence. In V. Cook and W. Li (Eds.), *The Cambridge handbook of linguistic multi-competence* (pp. 1–25). Cambridge: Cambridge University Press. https://doi.org/10.1017/cbo9781107425965.001.

Cook, V. (2022). Multi-competence and translanguaging. In J. MacSwan (Eds.), *Multilingual perspectives on translanguaging* (pp. 45–65).New York: Multilingual Matters. https://doi.org/10.21832/9781800415690-004.

Creese, A., and Blackledge, A. (2010). Translanguaging in the bilingual classroom: A pedagogy for learning and teaching? *Modern Language Journal*, *94*(1), 103–115. https://doi.org/10.1111/j.1540-4781.2009.00986.x.

Cushman, E. (2016). Translingual and decolonial approaches to meaning making. *College English*, *78*(3), 234–242.

De Costa, P., Singh, J., Milu, E. *et al.* (2017). Pedagogizing translingual practice: Prospects and possibilities. *Research in the Teaching of English*, *51*(4), 464–472.

De los Ríos, C. V., and Seltzer, K. (2017). Translanguaging, coloniality, and English classrooms: An exploration of two bicoastal urban classrooms. *Research in the Teaching of English*, *52*(1), 55–76. www.jstor.org/stable/44821287.

Domke, L. M. (2023). How children read multilingual texts: A description of reading translanguaging strategies. *Applied Linguistics*, https://doi.org/10.1093/applin/amad032.

Dovchin, S. (2021). Translanguaging, emotionality, and English as a second language immigrants: Mongolian background women in Australia. *TESOL Quarterly*, *55*, 839–865. https://doi.org/10.1002/tesq.3015.

Dovchin, S., and Dryden, S. (2022). Translingual discrimination: Skilled transnational migrants in the labour market of Australia. *Applied Linguistics*, *43*(2), 365–388. https://doi.org/10.1093/applin/amab041.

Dryer, D. (2016). Appraising translingualism. *College English*, *78*(3), 274–283.

Du, Q., Kim, H. R., Lee, J. W., *et al.* (2020). With or without translingualism. In T. Silva, and Z. Wang (Eds.), *Reconciling translingualism and second language writing* (pp. 210–224). New York: Routledge. https://doi.org/10.4324/9781003003786-22.

Ene, E., McIntosh, K., and Connor, U. (2019). Using intercultural rhetoric to examine translingual practices of postgraduate L2 writers of English. *Journal of Second Language Writing*, *45*, 105–110. https://doi.org/10.1016/j.jslw.2019.100664.

Eren, Ö. (2022). Towards multilingual turn in language classes: Plurilingual awareness as an indicator of intercultural communicative competence. *International Journal of Multilingualism*, 1–19. https://doi.org/10.1080/14790718.2022.2090568.

Ferris, D. (2014). "English only" and multilingualism in composition studies: Policy, philosophy, and practice (Book Review). *College English*, *77*(1), 73–83.

Flores, N. (2013). The unexamined relationship between neoliberalism and plurilingualism: A cautionary tale. *TESOL Quarterly*, *47*(3), 500–520. https://doi.org/10.1002/tesq.114.

Flores, N., and Aneja, G. (2017). "Why needs hiding?": Translingual (re)orientations in TESOL teacher education. *Research in the Teaching of English*, *51*(4), 441–463.

García, O. (2009). *Bilingual education in the 21st century: A global perspective*. Malden, MA: Wiley-Blackwell.

García, O., and Kleifgen, J. A. (2020). Translanguaging and Literacies. *Reading Research Quarterly*, *55*(4), 553–571. https://doi.org/10.1002/rrq.286.

García, O., and Li, W. (2014). *Translanguaging: Language, bilingualism and education*. New York: Palgrave Pivot.

García, O., Flores, N., Seltzer, K. *et al.* (2021). Rejecting abyssal thinking in the language and education of racialized bilinguals: A manifesto. *Critical Inquiry in Language Studies*, *18*(3), 203–228. https://doi.org/10.1080/15427587.2021.1935957.

García, O., Johnson, S., and Seltzer, K. (2017). *The translanguaging classroom: Leveraging student bilingualism for learning*. Philadelphia: Caslon. https://doi.org/10.21283/2376905x.9.165.

Gevers, J. (2018). Translingualism revisited: Language difference and hybridity in L2 writing. *Journal of Second Language Writing*, *40*, 73–83. https://doi.org/10.1016/j.jslw.2018.04.003.

Gilyard, K. (2016). The rhetoric of translingualism. *College English*, *78*(3), 284–289.

Gong, Y., Lyu, D., and Gao, X. (2018). Research on teaching Chinese as a second or foreign language in and outside mainland China: A bibliometric analysis. *Asian-Pacifific Education Research*. 27, 277–289. https://doi.org/10.1007/s40299-018-0385-2.

Guerra, J. C. (2016). Cultivating a rhetorical sensibility in the translingual writing classroom. *College English*, *78*(3), 228–233.

Guo, L., Xu, F., Feng, Z., and Zhang, G. (2016). A bibliometric analysis of oyster research from 1991 to 2014. *Aquaculture International*, *24*(1), 327–344. https://doi.org/10.1007/s10499-015-9928-1.

Hamman, L. (2018). Translanguaging and positioning in two-way dual language classrooms: A case for criticality. *Language and Education*, *32*(1), 21–42. https://doi.org/10.1080/09500782.2017.1384006.

Hawkins, M. (2018). Transmodalities and transnational encounters: Fostering critical cosmopolitan relations. *Applied Linguistics*, *39*(1), 55–77. https://doi.org/10.1093/applin/amx048.

Hirvela, A., and Belcher, D. (2016). Reading/writing and speaking/writing connections: The advantages of multimodal pedagogy. In R. Manchón, and P. K. Matsuda (Eds.), *Handbook of second and foreign language writing* (pp. 587–612). Berlin: de Gruyter. https://doi.org/10.1515/9781614511335-030.

Horner, B. (2001). "Students' Right," English only, and re-imagining the politics of language. *College English*, *63*(6), 741–758. https://doi.org/10.2307/1350100.

Horner, B. (2011). Relocating basic writing. *Journal of Basic Writing*, *30*(2), 5–23. https://doi.org/10.37514/jbw-j.2011.30.2.02.

Horner, B. (2017). Teaching translingual agency in iteration: Rewriting difference. In B. Horner, and L. Tetreault (Eds.), *Crossing divides: Exploring translingual writing pedagogies and programs* (pp. 87–97). Boulder, CO: Utah State University Press. https://doi.org/10.7330/9781607326205.c005.

Horner, B. (2018). Translinguality and disciplinary reinvention. *Across the Disciplines, 15*(3), 76–88. https://doi.org/10.37514/atd-j.2018.15.3.13.

Horner, B., and Tetreault, L. (2016). Translation as (global) writing. *Composition Studies, 44*(1), 13–30.

Horner, B., and Tetreault, L. (2017). Introduction. In B. Horner, and L. Tetreault (Eds.), *Crossing divides: Exploring translingual writing pedagogies and programs* (pp. 3–16). Boulder, CO: Utah State University Press. https://doi .org/10.7330/9781607326205.c000.

Horner, B., and Trimbur, J. (2002). English only and U.S. college composition. *College Composition and Communication, 53*(4), 594–630. https://doi.org/ 10.2307/1512118.

Horner, B., Lu, M-Z., and Matsuda, P. K. (Eds.) (2010). *Cross-language relations in composition.* Carbondale, IL: Southern Illinois University Press.

Horner, B., Lu, M-Z., Jones Royster, J., and Trimbur, J. (2011). Language difference in writing: Toward a translingual approach. *College English, 73* (3), 303–321.

Horner, B., NeCamp, S., and Donahue, C. (2011). Toward a multilingual composition scholarship: From English only to a translingual norm. *College Composition and Communication, 63*(2), 269–300.

Hyland, K. (2007). Genre pedagogy: Language, literacy and L2 writing instruction. *Journal of Second Language Writing, 16*(3), 148–164. https://doi .org/10.1016/j.jslw.2007.07.005.

Hyland, K., and Jiang, F. (2021). A bibliometric study of EAP research: Who is doing what, where and when? *Journal of English for Academic Purposes, 49*, 100929.

Jain, R. (2014). Global Englishes, translingual identities, and translingual practices in a community college ESL classroom: A practitioner researcher reports. *TESOL Journal, 5*(3), 490–522. https://doi.org/10.1002/tesj.155.

Kafle, M. (2020). "No one would like to take a risk": Multilingual students' views on language mixing in academic writing. *System, 94*, 102326. https:// doi.org/10.1016/j.system.2020.102326.

Kato, R., and Kumagai, Y. (2022). Translingual practices in a "monolingual" society: Discourses, learners' subjectivities and language choices. *International Journal of Bilingual Education and Bilingualism, 25*(5), 1681–1696. https://doi .org/10.1080/13670050.2020.1799318.

Kilfoil, C. B. (2015). Beyond the "foreign" language requirement: From a monolingual to a translingual ideology in rhetoric and composition.

Rhetoric Review, *34*(4), 426–444. https://doi.org/10.1080/07350198.2015.1073560.

Kim, K. M., and Park, G. (2020). "It is more expressive for me": A translingual approach to meaningful literacy instruction through Sijo poetry. *TESOL Quarterly*, *54*(2), 281–309. https://doi.org/10.1002/tesq.545.

Kim, S., and Chang, C.-H. (2022). Japanese L2 learners' translanguaging practice in written peer feedback. *International Journal of Bilingual Education and Bilingualism*, *25*(4), 1363–1376. https://doi.org/10.1080/13670050.2020.1760201.

Kramsch, C. (2018). Trans-spatial utopias. *Applied Linguistics*, *39*(1), 108–115. https://doi.org/10.1093/applin/amx057.

Kubota, R. (2016). The multi/plural turn, postcolonial theory, and neoliberal multiculturalism: Complicities and implications for applied linguistics. *Applied Linguistics*, *37*(4), 474–494. https://doi.org/10.1093/applin/amu045.

Kuteeva, M. (2020). Revisiting the "E" in EMI: Students' perceptions of standard English, lingua franca and translingual practices. *International Journal of Bilingual Education and Bilingualism*, *23*(3), 287–300. https://doi.org/10.1080/13670050.2019.1637395.

Lam, R. (2015). Convergence and divergence of process and portfolio approaches to L2 writing instruction: Issues and implications. *RELC Journal*, *46*(3), 293–308. https://doi.org/10.1177/0033688215597119.

Lan, G., Zhang, Q., Lucas, K., Sun, Y., and Gao, J. (2022). A corpus-based investigation on noun phrase complexity in L1 and L2 English writing. *English for Specific Purposes*, *67*, 4–17. https://doi.org/10.1016/j.esp.2022.02.002.

Lee, J. (2016). Beyond translingual writing. *College English*, *79*(2), 174–195.

Lee, J., and Jenks, C. (2016). Doing translingual dispositions. *College Composition and Communication*, *68*(2), 317–344.

Lei, L., and Liu, D. (2019a). Research trends in applied linguistics from 2005 to 2016: A bibliometric analysis and its implications. *Applied Linguistics*, *40*(3), 540–561. https://doi.org/10.1093/applin/amy003.

Lei, L., and Liu, D. (2019b). The research trends and contributions of System's publications over the past four decades (1973–2017): A bibliometric analysis. *System*, *80*(3), 1–13. https://doi.org/10.1016/j.system.2018.10.003.

Leonard, R. L., and Nowacek, R. (2016). Transfer and translingualism. *College English* *78*(3), 258–264.

Li, W. (2018). Translanguaging as a practical theory of language. *Applied Linguistics*, *39*(1), 9–30. https://doi.org/10.1093/applin/amx039.

Li, W., and García, O. (2022). Not a first language but one repertoire: Translanguaging as a decolonizing project. *RELC Journal*, *53*(2), 313–324. https://doi.org/10.1177/00336882221092841.

Li, W., and Ho, W. Y. (2018). Language learning sans frontiers: A translanguaging view. *Annual Review of Applied Linguistics, 38*, 33–59. https://doi.org/10.1017/S0267190518000053.

Li, W., and Zhu, H. (2013). Translanguaging identities and ideologies: Creating transnational space through flexible multilingual practices amongst Chinese university students in the UK. *Applied Linguistics, 34*(5), 516–535. https://doi.org/10.1093/applin/amt022.

Liao, S., and Lei, L. (2017). What we talk about when we talk about corpus: A bibliometric analysis of corpus-related research in linguistics (2000–2015). *Glottometrics, 38*, 1–20.

Lin, Z., and Lei, L. (2020). The research trends of multilingualism in applied linguistics and education (2000–2019): A bibliometric analysis. *Sustainability, 12*(15), 1–14. https://doi.org/10.3390/su12156058.

Liu, L. H. (1995). *Translingual practice: Literature, national culture, and translated modernity – China, 1900–1937*. California: Stanford University Press.

Llanes, À., and Cots, J. M. (2022). Measuring the impact of translanguaging in TESOL: A plurilingual approach to ESP. *International Journal of Multilingualism, 19*(4), 523–538. https://doi.org/10.1080/14790718.2020.1753749.

Llinares, A., and Evnitskaya, N. (2021). Classroom interaction in CLIL programs: Offering opportunities or fostering inequalities? *TESOL Quarterly, 55*(2), 366–397. https://doi.org/10.1002/tesq.607.

Lu, M-Z. (1994). Professing multiculturalism: The politics of style in the contact zone. *College Composition and Communication, 45*(4), 442–458. https://doi.org/10.2307/358759.

Lu, M-Z., and Horner, B. (2013). Translingual literacy, language difference, and matters of agency. *College English, 75*(6), 582–611.

Lu, M-Z., and Horner, B. (2016). Introduction: Translingual work. *College English, 78*(3), 207–218.

Lu, X. (2017). Automated measurement of syntactic complexity in corpus-based L2 writing research and implications for writing assessment. *Language Testing, 34*(4), 493–511. https://doi.org/10.1177/0265532217710675.

MacSwan, J. (2017). A multilingual perspective on translanguaging. *American Educational Research Journal, 54*(1), 167–201. https://doi.org/10.3102/0002831216683935.

MacSwan, J. (2022). *Multilingual perspectives on translanguaging*. New York: Multilingual Matters.

Manchón, R. (2016). Language and L2 writing: Learning to write and writing to learn in academic contexts. In K. Hyland and P. Shaw (Eds.), *Handbook of*

English for Academic Purpose (pp. 139–151). London: Routledge. https://doi.org/10.1515/9781614511335-005.

Manchón, R., and Williams, J. (2016). L2 writing and SLA studies. In R. Manchón, and P. K. Matsuda (Eds.), *Handbook of second and foreign language writing* (pp. 567–586). Berlin: de Gruyter. https://doi.org/10.1515/9781614511335-029.

Matsuda, P. K. (1999). Composition studies and ESL writing: A disciplinary division of labor. *College Composition and Communication, 50*(4), 699–721. https://doi.org/10.2307/358488.

Matsuda, P. K. (2003). Basic writing and second language writers: Toward an inclusive definition. *Journal of Basic Writing, 22*(2), 67–89. https://doi.org/10.37514/jbw-j.2003.22.2.05.

Matsuda, P. K. (2013). It's the wild west out there: A new linguistic frontier in U.S. composition. In A. S. Canagarajah (Ed.), *Literacy as translingual practice: Between communities and classrooms* (pp. 128–138), New York: Routledge. https://doi.org/10.4324/9780203120293-19.

Matsuda, P. K. (2014). The lure of translingual writing. *PMLA, 129*(3), 478–483.

Milson-Whyte, V. (2013). Pedagogical and sociopolitical implications of code-meshing in classrooms: Some considerations for a translingual orientation to writing. In A. S. Canagarajah (Ed.), *Literacy as translingual practice: Between communities and classrooms* (pp. 115–127), New York: Routledge. https://doi.org/10.4324/9780203120293-18.

Nishino, T., and Atkinson, D. (2015). Second language writing as sociocognitive alignment. *Journal of Second Language Writing, 27*, 37–54. https://doi.org/10.1016/j.jslw.2014.11.002.

Ochs, E., Schegloff, E., and Thompson, S. A. (1996). *Interaction and grammar.* Cambridge: Cambridge University Press.

Ollerhead, S., Crealy, I., and Kirk, R. (2020). "Writing like a health scientist": A translingual approach to teaching text structure in a diverse Australian classroom. *Australian Journal of Applied Linguistics, 3*, 77–90. https://doi.org/10.29140/ajal.v3n1.301.

Ortega, L. (2012). Epilogue: Exploring L2 writing-SLA interfaces. *Journal of Second Language Writing, 21*(4), 404–415. https://doi.org/10.1016/j.jslw.2012.09.002.

Otheguy, R., García, O., and Reid, W. (2015). Clarifying translanguaging and deconstructing named languages: A perspective from linguistics. *Applied Linguistics Review, 6*(3), 281–307. https://doi.org/10.1515/applirev-2015-0014.

Pacheco, M. B., Daniel, S. M., Pray, L. C., and Jiménez, R. T. (2019). Translingual practice, strategic participation, and meaning-making. *Journal of Literacy Research*, *51*(1), 75–99. https://doi.org/10.1177/1086296×188 20642.

Pennycook, A., and Otsuji, E. (2015). *Metrolingualism: Language in the city*. Abingdon: Routledge.

Poza, L. (2017). Translanguaging: Definitions, implications, and further needs in burgeoning inquiry. *Berkeley Review of Education*, *6*(2), 101–128. https://doi.org/10.5070/B86110060.

Pratt, M. L. (1991). Arts of the contact zone. *Profession*, *91*, 33–40.

Pratt, M. L., Geisler, M., Kramsch, C. *et al.* (2008). Transforming college and university foreign language departments. *Modern Language Journal*, *92*(2), 287–293. https://doi.org/10.1111/j.1540-4781.2007.00719_2.x.

Pritchard, A. (1969). Statistical bibliography or bibliometrics? *Journal of Documentation*, *25*(4), 348–349.

Rafi, A. S. M., and Morgan, A.-M. (2023). Blending translanguaging and CLIL: Pedagogical benefits and ideological challenges in a Bangladeshi classroom. *Critical Inquiry in Language Studies*, *20*(1), 20–45. https://doi.org/10.1080/15427587.2022.2090361.

Rinnert, C., and Kobayashi, H. (2016). Multicompetence and multilingual writing. In R. Manchón, and P. K. Matsuda (Eds.), *Handbook of second and foreign language writing* (pp. 366–385). Berlin: de Gruyter. https://doi.org/10.1515/9781614511335-020.

Sah, P. K., and Kubota, R. (2022). Towards critical translanguaging: A review of literature on English as a medium of instruction in South Asia's school education. *Asian Englishes*, *24*(2), 132–146. https://doi.org/10.1080/13488678.2022.2056796.

Sato, E., and García, O. (2023). Translanguaging, translation and interpreting studies, and bilingualism. In A. Ferreira, and J. W. Schwieter (Eds.), *The Routledge handbook of translation, interpreting and bilingualism* (pp. 328–345). New York: Routledge. https://doi.org/10.4324/9781003109020-27.

Schreiber, B. R. (2015). "I Am What I Am": Multilingual identity and digital translanguaging. *Language Learning & Technology*, *19*(3), 69–87. http://dx.doi.org/10125/44434.

Schreiber, B. R., and Watson, M. (2018). Translingualism ≠ code-meshing: A response to Gevers' "translingualism revisited" (2018). *Journal of Second Language Writing*, *42*, 94–97. https://doi.org/10.1016/j.jslw.2018.10.007.

Seltzer, K. (2020). "My English is its own rule": Voicing a translingual sensibility through poetry. *Journal of Language, Identity, and Education*, *19*(5), 297–311. https://doi.org/10.1080/15348458.2019.1656535.

Severino, C. (2017). "Multilingualizing" composition: A diary self-study of learning Spanish and Chinese. *Composition Studies*, *45*(2), 12–31.

Shi, J. G., Miao, W., and Si, H. (2019). Visualization and analysis of mapping knowledge domain of urban vitality research. *Sustainability, 11*(4), 1–17. https://doi.org/10.3390/su11040988.

Silva, T. (1997). On the ethical treatment of ESL writers. *TESOL Quarterly, 31* (2), 359–363. https://doi.org/10.2307/3588052.

Silva, T., and Leki, I. (2004). Family matters: The influence of applied linguistics and composition studies on second language writing studies – past, present, and future. *Modern Language Journal, 88*(1), 1–13. https://doi.org/10.1111/j.0026-7902.2004.00215.x.

Silva, T., Leki, I., and Carson, J. (1997). Broadening the perspective of mainstream composition studies: Some thoughts from the disciplinary margins. *Written Communication, 14*(3), 398–428. https://doi.org/10.1177/07410 88397014003004.

Smith, B. E., Pacheco, M. B., and De Almeida, C. R. (2017). Multimodal codemeshing: Bilingual adolescents' processes composing across modes and languages. *Journal of Second Language Writing, 36*, 6–22. https://doi .org/10.1016/j.jslw.2017.04.001.

Steele, C., Dovchin, S., and Oliver, R. (2022). "Stop measuring black kids with a white stick": Translanguaging for classroom assessment. *RELC Journal, 53* (2), 400–415. https://doi.org/10.1177/00336882221086307.

Sun, P., and Zhang, L. J. (2022). Effects of translanguaging in online peer feedback on Chinese university English-as-a-foreign-language students' second language writing performance. *RELC Journal, 53*(2), 325–341. https://doi.org/10.1177/ 00336882221089051.

Sun X., Wang P., and Qin, Y. (2024): Twenty years' development of translanguaging: A bibliometric analysis, *International Journal of Multilingualism, 21*(1), 209. https://doi.org/10.1080/14790718.2021.2007933.

Sun, Y. (2022). Implementation of translingual pedagogies in EAL writing: A systematic review. *Language Teaching Research*.136216882210906. https://doi.org/10.1177/13621688221090665.

Sun, Y. (2023). Increasing critical language awareness through translingual practices in academic writing. *Journal of English for Academic Purposes, 62*, 101229. https://doi.org/10.1016/j.jeap.2023.101229.

Sun, Y., and Lan, G. (2021a). Enactment of a translingual approach to writing. *TESOL Quarterly, 55*(2), 398–426. https://doi.org/10.1002/tesq.609.

Sun, Y., and Lan, G. (2021b). Research trends in "trans-" studies on writing: A bibliometric analysis. *System, 103*, 102640. https://doi.org/10.1016/j.system .2021.102640.

Sun, Y., and Lan, G. (2023). A bibliometric analysis on L2 writing in the first 20 years of the 21st century: Research impacts and research trends. *Journal of*

Second Language Writing, 59, 100963. https://doi.org/10.1016/j.jslw.2023 .100963.

Sun, Y., Lan, G., and Zhang, L. (2023). Pedagogical values of translingual practices in improving student feedback literacy in academic writing. *Assessing Writing, 56*, 100715. https://doi.org/10.1016/j.asw.2023.100715.

Sun Y., Yang K., and Silva T. (2021) Multimodality in L2 writing: Intellectual roots and contemporary developments. In D. Shin, T. Cimasko, and Y. Yi (Eds.), *Multimodal composing in K-16 ESL and EFL education* (pp. 3–16). Singapore: Springer. https://doi-org.proxy.lib.duke.edu/10.1007/978-981-16-0530-7_1.

Tai, K. W. H., and Li, W. (2021). Constructing playful talk through translanguaging in English medium instruction mathematics classrooms. *Applied Linguistics, 42*(4), 607–640. https://doi.org/10.1093/applin/amaa043.

Tai, K. W. H., and Wong, C. (2023). Empowering students through the construction of a translanguaging space in an English as a first language classroom. *Applied Linguistics, 44*(6), 1100–1151. https://doi.org/10.1093/applin/amac069.

Tannenbaum, M. (2014). "With a tongue forked in two": Translingual Arab writers in Israel. *International Journal of Bilingualism, 18*(2), 99–117. https://doi.org/10.1177/1367006912458393.

Tardy, C. M. (2017). Crossing, or creating, divides? A plea for transdisciplinary scholarship. In B. Horner, and L. Tetreault (Eds.), *Crossing divides: Exploring translingual writing pedagogies and programs* (pp. 181–189). Boulder, CO: Utah State University Press. https://doi.org/10.7330/9781607326205.c010.

Tardy, C. M., and Whittig, E. (2017). On the ethical treatment of EAL writers: An update. *TESOL Quarterly, 51*(4), 920–931. https://doi.org/10.1002/tesq.405.

Trimbur, J. (2016). Translingualism and close reading. *College English, 78*(3), 219–227.

Turner, M., and Lin, A. M. Y. (2020). Translanguaging and named languages: Productive tension and desire. *International Journal of Bilingual Education and Bilingualism, 23*(4), 423–433. https://doi.org/10.1080/13670050.2017.1360243.

Velasco, P., and García, O. (2014). Translanguaging and the writing of bilingual learners. *Bilingual Research Journal, 37*(1), 6–23. https://doi.org/10.1080/15235882.2014.893270.

Waltman, L., Van Eck, N. J., and Noyons, E. C. M. (2010). A unified approach to mapping and clustering of bibliometric networks. *Journal of Informetrics, 4*(4), 629–635. https://doi.org/10.48550/arxiv.1006.1032.

Wible, S. (2013). *Shaping language policy in the U. S.: The role of composition studies*. Carbondale: Southern Illinois University Press.

Williams, C. (1994). *Arfarniad o Ddulliau Dysgu ac Addysgu yng Nghyddestun Addysg Uwchradd Ddwyieithog* [An evaluation of teaching and learning methods in the context of bilingual secondary education] (Unpublished doctoral dissertation). University of Wales, Bangor, UL.

Worden, D. (2018). Balancing stability and flexibility in genre-based writing instruction: A case study of a novice L2 writing teacher. *Journal of Second Language Writing*, *42*, 44–57. https://doi.org/10.1016/j.jslw.2018.09.003.

Xie, D., and Sun, Y. (2023). Pedagogical implications of translingual practices for content and language integrated learning. *Applied Linguistics Review*, https://doi.org/10.1515/applirev-2023-0057.

You, X. (2010). *Writing in the devil's tongue: A history of English composition in China*. Carbondale: Southern Illinois University Press.

Young, V. A. (2004). Your average nigga. *College Composition and Communication*, *55*(4), 693–715. https://doi.org/10.2307/4140667.

Zamel, V. (1983). The composing processes of advanced ESL students: Six case studies. *TESOL Quarterly*, *17*(2), 165–187. https://doi.org/10.2307/3586647.

Zhang-Wu, Q., and Tian, Z. (2023). Raising critical language awareness in a translanguaging infused teacher education course: Opportunities and challenges. *Journal of Language, Identity, and Education*, *22*(4), 376–395. https://doi.org/10.1080/15348458.2023.2202589.

Cambridge Elements ⁼

Applied Linguistics

Li Wei
University College London

Li Wei is Chair of Applied Linguistics at the UCL Institute of Education, University College London (UCL), and Fellow of Academy of Social Sciences, UK. His research covers different aspects of bilingualism and multilingualism. He was the founding editor of the following journals: *International Journal of Bilingualism* (Sage), *Applied Linguistics Review* (De Gruyter), *Language, Culture and Society* (Benjamins), *Chinese Language and Discourse* (Benjamins) and *Global Chinese* (De Gruyter), and is currently Editor of the *International Journal of Bilingual Education and Bilingualism* (Taylor and Francis). His books include the *Blackwell Guide to Research Methods in Bilingualism and Multilingualism* (with Melissa Moyer) and *Translanguaging: Language, Bilingualism and Education* (with Ofelia Garcia) which won the British Association of Applied Linguistics Book Prize.

Zhu Hua
University College London

Zhu Hua is Professor of Language Learning and Intercultural Communication at the UCL Institute of Education, University College London (UCL) and is a Fellow of Academy of Social Sciences, UK. Her research is centred around multilingual and intercultural communication. She has also studied child language development and language learning. She is book series co-editor for *Routledge Studies in Language and Intercultural Communication* and *Cambridge Key Topics in Applied Linguistics*, and Forum and Book Reviews Editor of *Applied Linguistics* (Oxford University Press).

About the Series

Mirroring the Cambridge Key Topics in Applied Linguistics, this Elements series focuses on the key topics, concepts and methods in Applied Linguistics today. It revisits core conceptual and methodological issues in different subareas of Applied Linguistics. It also explores new emerging themes and topics. All topics are examined in connection with real-world issues and the broader political, economic and ideological contexts.

.

Cambridge Elements ≡

Applied Linguistics

Printed in the United States
by Baker & Taylor Publisher Services